Aren't the Emperor's

New Clothes Grand

Philip M. Fishman

Foreword by Susan Wright

AREN'T THE EMPEROR'S NEW CLOTHES GRAND

Philip M. Fishman

Foreword by Susan Wright

Aren't The Emperor's New Clothes Grand

Copyright 2018 Philip M. Fishman

ISBN: 978-09891708-2-6

Published by MPS Publishing

Table of Contents

Foreword

I was honored and delighted when Phil Fishman asked me to provide the foreword to his book. His book and title perfectly characterize the Trump Cult and their love of fake news. He refers to a type of mass hypnosis to explain the phenomena; and as conspiratorial as it sounds, I'm not sure that there is any other rational explanation.

It's like waking up and finding that our country has fallen down a very deep rabbit hole. Many of us would never have guessed where this media-driven culture would eventually take us, but here we are – a nation being led by the buffoonish whims of a reality TV host. The Republican Party's reputation and relevance are on the line, as they've trusted Donald Trump – the same man whose brand has failed over and over, whether with vodka or casinos – to be the new brand of the GOP.

Fishman's latest effort dares to step out of the crowd of sycophants and declare, "The orange emperor is naked, guys!"

Before we throw a Trump Hotel robe over this squeamish period in our history, allow Fishman to take you step-by-step through who Trump is, and how the nation became his latest acquisition.

Susan Wright

Introduction

In Hans Christian Andersen's tale, *The Emperor's New Clothes,* two unscrupulous tailors appeal to the emperor's vanity by offering to make him a suit of clothes that would be woven of such fine fiber that it would be invisible to all those who were unworthy of seeing it. (And, I guess so light in weight that the wearer would not be able to feel it.) When the proud emperor paraded out in his birthday suit; his subjects exclaimed how grand the emperor's new clothes were. All except a young child who stated the obvious.

The tone of the story suggests that the people were not deceived; but only went along with the ruse. What is not clear is if Trump's followers are likewise undeceived at his obvious equivocating, and are consciously apologizing for him; or if they have somehow succumbed to a type of mass hypnosis.

It may be akin to mass hysteria, which is well understood. When someone shouts "Fire" in a theater; whether true or not, otherwise rational people, almost spontaneously, begin to act irrationally. Typically, many more people are injured and killed than if people evacuated the premises in an orderly manner.

A book written by a German psychiatrist in 1933[1] is eerily prescient of what appears to be going on today with respect to Trump's cult. Trump stated during the campaign that he could shoot someone on Fifth Avenue and not lose any support. From the many comments that I saw on FaceBook, it appears that he was right. Instead of outrage among his followers that he was in essence referring to them as lemmings; most of them thought it was funny. One suggested that he shoot Hillary Clinton, and another thought it would be a good idea to shoot a number of

Democrats as well as RINOS (the acronym for Republicans in name only).

What could possibly account for this phenomena? What could explain large numbers of people being so fed up with the corruption, lying, and broken promises in Washington that they would elect someone whose personal resume reads like a primer in deceit?

In the fore mentioned book by Wilhelm Reich he refers to the "little man", who feels so subjugated by the establishment that he wants to rebel; but ironically is drawn to the authoritarian who promises to reform the system, or in Trump's language, "drain the swamp".

Part I
The Man

Chapter 1 Military

Donald Trump loves the military. He attended military prep school and probably fancied himself a general. In April 2016, during a Meet the Press interview when he was asked about his qualifications to be Commander-in-Chief, he responded, *"I will be so good at the military, your head will spin."*

Another time during the campaign, he actually said that he knew more than the generals about ISIS. Now, ironically, he is Commander in Chief over all the generals. Surely, he would love a uniform bedecked with all the medals he never earned as a consequence of dodging the draft. OK, four of those deferments were legitimate college deferments; but the deferment that got him off permanently was the diagnosis of bone spurs in his feet. That sounds awfully serious. Can you imagine a soldier with bone spurs able to function? But, over the years, the bone spurs must have miraculously healed; because at the age of seventy, he often plays tennis and golf.

Trump's love of the military reveals itself in several ways; he really loves veterans so long as they are not homeless and loitering in front of Trump Tower. Perhaps, they were just hoping to get a job from the great Employer; but if that's the case, why didn't they just wheel in and ask for a job interview? One can only imagine what his response would have been, given what he wrote back in 1991, reported by Red State:

"While disabled veterans should be given every opportunity to earn a living, is it fair to do so to the detriment of the city as a whole or its tax paying citizens and businesses? Do we allow Fifth Ave., one of the world's finest and most luxurious shopping districts, to be turned into an outdoor flea market, clogging and seriously downgrading the area?"

And then the following letter to Mayor Bloomberg in 2004.

"Whether they are veterans or not, [they] should not be allowed to sell on this most important and prestigious shopping street. The image of New York City will suffer. I hope you can stop this very deplorable situation before it is too late."

Trump also has a problem with POWs, given his disparaging words about Senator John McCain. According to our fearless leader; you shouldn't allow yourself to be captured. Go down fighting; but never surrender. Or, just don't put yourself in a situation, where you might be captured. Trump sure had that one figured out.

Chapter 2 Leadership

Tying into the previous chapter, Trump sees himself as a leader of men (and women). Unfortunately, he apparently often confuses the difference between leadership of a nation and the position of a boss in the business world. While both types of leaders have goals that they want their subordinates to accomplish, the methods a boss uses to achieve those goals determine if he is also a leader. A leader leads by inspiring his team, setting examples and developing similar goals for them. He leads by example, and Trump's examples only draw more good people on his team into a growing net of despicable behaviors.

A leader abides by President Harry S. Truman's famous bromide, *"The buck stops here."*, and uses *I,* instead of *you* or *they* when there is a screw-up. When something is done well, he never takes personal credit; and is more likely to use the word *you* or *we.* The subordinates' view of their boss tells the story. If it is one of respect and trust; then the boss is a leader. If on the other hand; it is one of fear and distrust, the boss is only a boss who may wonder at times why his people aren't more loyal.

Nothing much of significance had gotten passed through most of Trump's first year in office, (other than the tax reform bill, which will be discussed in a later chapter) despite the House, Senate, and White House all being controlled by the same party — Republicans. But, according to Trump; he is not to blame.

"We're not getting the job done. And I'm not going to blame myself, I'll be honest,"[1] Without much of a pause, Trump amended his statement from 'we' to 'they'. *"They're not getting the job done,"* he repeated.

A good quarterback on a football team is a leader. When the team scores; even if it's a result of his eluding tacklers from some missed blocks, he congratulates the team. If the missed blocks result in his being tackled for a loss, he doesn't cast blame. Trump appears to be a different kind of quarterback, a razzle dazzle quarterback. A quarterback that loves the razzle dazzle; but never bothered to learn the playbook or the rules. Occasionally, one of those razzle dazzle plays gains a lot of yards; but somehow the team hardly ever scores. Of course, it's always the fault of one or more of his teammates, or the referees when the play fails. The quarterback just doesn't understand that some of the simplest plays actually score and win games.

And, a leader can sure deliver some inspiring speeches. Speaking at the 2017 Boy Scout Jamboree in West Virginia, he began well enough by saying that he would refrain from injecting politics into his speech; but couldn't even end his sentence without a subtle dig at the free press. "*...put aside all of the policy fights you've been hearing about with the fake news and all that...*" Apparently, fake news is such an important point for our young people to hear that Trump needs to repeat it. He's able to do that when he talks about crowd size and poor media coverage. "*Boy, you have a lot of people here. The press will say it's about 200 people. It looks like about 45,000 people. You set a record today...*"

Exaggerated crowd size is a recurring theme at many of Trump's appearances. According to the official Boy Scout estimate, there were about 40,000 present. 1960 holds the record at 56,000. He had also exclaimed about the record setting crowd at his inauguration, although photographs showed that attendance was about half that of Obama's first inauguration.

The size of the crowd and fake news was obviously a very important part of this inspiring speech, since he went back to it later. "*... Man, this is a lot of people. Turn those cameras back* *there, please. That is so incredible... what do you think the chances are that this incredible massive crowd, record setting, is going to be shown on television tonight? One percent or zero? The fake media will say, "President Trump spoke" — you know what is — "President Trump spoke before a small crowd of Boy Scouts today." That's some — that is some crowd. Fake media. Fake news."*

And, just to make sure that his point had been absorbed, he returned to the theme again when he spoke about election night and the polls that had been so wrong: Fake news, of course.

But, with all that said; we wouldn't want to convey the impression that Trump had ignored scouting values in his speech. After mentioning several of his appointees who had been scouts, and two who had achieved the rank of Eagle Scout; he went on to say that *"Boy Scout values are American values. And, great Boy Scouts become great, great Americans. As the Scout law says, a scout is trustworthy, loyal — we could use some more loyalty I will tell that you that." It* would have been nice to expound a little on trustworthiness; but we must assume that Mr. Trump was pressed for time.

Chapter 3 The Businessman

"Life hasn't been easy..." After being turned down repeatedly, Trump's father finally gave him a *"small loan"* of about a million dollars to start his business. But he had to *"pay it back with interest"*.[1] Who can deny Donald Trump's reputation as an astute businessman? Who else could have turned a measly million into a reported seven billion, or two or three billion or whatever?

There is no doubt as to Trump's reputation; but that begs the question. Is that reputation deserved? Donald may have thought he had it rough early on; but he possibly forgot the inheritance from his father.

In 1974, Fred Trump turned control of his company, then valued at $200 million over to Donald. When Fred died in 1999, Donald's share of the inheritance was one-fifth of Fred's estate. We can therefore slightly amend Trump's statement of a *"small loan"* of about a million dollars to receiving an inheritance in 1999, which was valued at $40 million in 1974. For some perspective, if that $40 million had been invested in the S&P 500 index in 1974; it would be worth about $1.6 billion today.

Even if that were acknowledged, Donald sells his father's contributions short. As important as the money was to launching his success, were the contacts and credibility that Fred bestowed on his son. Fred had cultivated a multitude of influential politicians and financiers over the years that is impossible to assign a monetary value on.

Nevertheless, Donald now has so much money that people (maybe, including Trump, himself) don't know the exact figure. Back in 2004, when he had applied for a loan with Deutsche

Bank to build Trump International Hotel & Tower in downtown Chicago, he had submitted unaudited financials showing a net worth of $3.5 billion. Deutsche Bank determined that that figure might be a slight exaggeration, and pegged his net worth at $788 million.[2]

The bank agreed to a $640 million loan with Trump posting a personal $40 million guarantee. Four years later after the collapse of the global real estate market, he attempted to renege on his personal guarantee and sued Deutsche Bank for $3 billion, claiming that Deutsche Bank and a consortium of lenders played a big part in the global real estate collapse. Deutsche Bank counter sued and eventually there was an undisclosed settlement.[3]

But that is not the end of the story. Despite his defaulting on the loan; Deutsche Bank and Trump have continued to do business. In June 2017, Trump disclosed outstanding loans from Deutche Bank against properties of at least $130 million; and according to people familiar with Trump's borrowings, may be closer to $300 million.[4]

How is that for business acumen? Defaulting on a loan, suing the lender, and then being able to get additional financing from that lender. That takes skill.

One thing that Donald learned very well at business school is leverage. He has said he loves leverage. That is the multiplier effect that you get when you use other people's money. And something he didn't need to learn in business school because it was instinctive; that multiplier effect becomes even larger when you don't pay back the loans.

But banks and investors are not the only ones that Trump has taken advantage of over the years. During the first Presidential debate of 2016, Hillary called on Donald to apologize for *"the thousands of people that you have stiffed over the course of your business"*; which tacitly asked if his habit of stiffing contractors was a characteristic that Americans should look for in a President.

She went on to say that she had met a number of people that had been cheated by Trump or his businesses, including *"dishwashers, painters, architects, glass installers, marble installers, drapery installers, like my dad was, who you refused to pay when they finished the work that you asked them to do."* She followed up by saying that she was glad that her father had never done business with Trump.[5] At least, we should credit Donald for not denying the accusations. He countered with something like they got lots of money; but if their work was not up to par, they didn't deserve the whole amount. Based on the large number of complaints, one might conclude that Trump must not have been too good at picking contractors.

In addition to those cited by Hillary in the debate, there were some sixty lawsuits, hundreds of liens, judgments and other government filings of plumbers, dozens of waiters, bartenders, and other hourly workers at Trump's resorts who have accused him of failing to pay them for their work. Real estate agents and even some lawyers that represented him in documenting the above were not exempt from being short-changed.[6]

Of course there were also a few bankruptcies along the way; but Trump is quick to point out that those were corporate bankruptcies; he personally has never declared bankruptcy. True enough. One might infer that he means that he was never among those who lost money from those bankruptcies.

But, wait. In a following chapter we will learn how he brilliantly (but legally) took advantage of the tax code in 1995 by declaring a $916 billion dollar loss. That apparently was not a result of a bankruptcy; so how did he manage to lose $916 billion? Maybe he just misplaced it.

In 1984, Donald decided that he wanted to be in sports big time. The USFL (United States Football League) had begun as a spring and summer time alternate professional league to the NFL with a great business concept. Since college and NFL football played in the fall; there would be no competition for the many fans who loved the sport. Each team would have first refusal on players from five colleges in their immediate area. The idea was to have a local flavor to each team to draw fans of those universities. And most important for financial survival was a salary cap. The league had been in business for a year when Donald, with no previous sport business experience purchased the New Jersey Generals.

Leave it to the intrepid entrepreneur to screw up a good concept. The Generals in their first year had a terrible won-loss record; and Donald was determined to fix that. Although there had been a covenant among the owners to abide by the salary cap; Donald felt that didn't apply to him since he wasn't one of the original signatories.

He proceeded to get into a bidding war with the NFL and ended up with some very good players. His coach came from the NFL; and the team performed very well (for two years). If the league had lasted, who knows; but Donald had grandiose ideas. His idea (probably from the start) was to move the schedule to the fall and compete directly with the NFL. This would supposedly force the NFL to seek a merger. Apparently, Donald had either forgotten or never learned a key principle of war in his days at military prep school. That principal is *mass,* defined as overwhelming power at a given place and time. The financial resources of the new league paled in comparison to the NFL, which had the overwhelming power. The result of the confrontation was predictable; and the league folded with the loss of millions of dollars.[7]

One would have thought that Donald had learned his lesson about getting into businesses that he knew nothing about. Nevertheless, he ventured into the airline business in 1989 by purchasing Eastern Shuttle, which operated a shuttle service between Boston, New York and Washington D.C. He would have been well advised to hire someone who knew something about the business. At the very least, surely he had learned in business school that market research is not a bad idea. His concept was to make the shuttle a luxury flight with all the trimmings and of course the added cost. What he would have learned with a little market research is that businessmen and women were not interested in luxury. All they wanted was to get from point A to point B as quickly and efficiently as possible. When his shuttle went bankrupt in 1992; he blamed it on the recession and was quoted,

"It was a great experience. I enjoyed it... It was incredibly well financed. That was the days where banks put up more than 100 percent of financing... I ran it really well, but the markets collapsed. ...airlines, real estate. Everything. It was the depression."[8]

After the airline washout, there were a series of business fiascos and over-hyped products including *Trump-the Game* (a *Monopoly* take off), *The Trump Network* (a multi-level marketing company to supposedly surpass Amway), *Trump Ice* (a supposedly luxury mineral water in a plastic bottle), *Trump Magazine* (a luxury quarterly that apparently was too luxurious for the luxury crowd).

In 2005, Donald got the itch to branch out again, with the announcement of Trump Super Premium Vodka, which strikes one as a bit peculiar, since Trump is a teetotaler. Nevertheless, the product made its entry in 2006 amid huge fanfare. He had told Larry King on Larry King Live that the reason he had gotten into vodka is that a close friend was the developer of *Grey Goose*, which many vodka connoisseurs considered the epitome of vodkas. Trump Vodka was going to top Grey Goose since he enjoyed beating the best. That's an idea for going into a given business that he didn't learn in business school- choose a business that one of your friends has excelled at; and show the world that you can do it better!

From all reports, Trump Vodka was an excellent vodka; but probably failed because of a combination of a financially weak distributor and price due to the glitzy bottle. The trademark was abandoned in 2008 and discontinued sales in the U.S. in 2011. An Israeli distributor has since been marketing the brand for use by Orthodox Jews at Passover; but even this small market appears to be in jeopardy due to a non-kosher ingredient found in some pre-2013 bottles which remain on store shelves.

Apparently, Trump had tired of getting into businesses that he knew nothing about; and decided to enter a business that he had quite a background in. In 2005, Trump got the brainstorm of an idea to start a training program for entrepreneurs in real estate. Who better to convey the message than the master of the art of the deal, Donald J. Trump himself? Thus, Trump University (also known as the Trump Wealth Institute and Trump Entrepreneur Initiative LLC) was born. After multiple lawsuits alleging fraud, the university folded in 2010. Although, Trump and his lawyers vigorously denied any wrong doing, two class action lawsuits were settled in 2016 for $25 million.[9]

Trump University was still in its infancy, when he decided to get into another business which fit his background. On April 5, 2006, Trump announced the launch of Trump Mortgage LLC, with the usual fanfare. Later that month, Trump appeared on CNBC and said,

"... it's a great time to start a mortgage company [...] the real estate market is going to be very strong for a long time to come."[10]

Sixteen months later, it was announced that the company would close due to poor economic conditions, etc. But, unsurprisingly, it was not Donald's fault. According to him, his role was limited to a name licensing deal. "The mortgage business is not a business I particularly liked or wanted to be part of in a very big way."[11] A few months before the announced closing of Trump Mortgage, the intrepid entrepreneur was at it again. Trump Steaks was launched to be sold initially by Sharper Image. Although he had no prior experience in the meat business, he felt it was a perfect fit. After all, with all those restaurants, his company was a big purchaser of steaks. However, after a three month trial, the contract was cancelled. The CEO of Sharper Image said that hardly any steaks were sold. [12]

That brings to mind an idea for the next Trump business. How about Trump Laundry? After all, his hotels do a lot of daily linen washing.

But, with all of his failings as an entrepreneur; he appears now to have achieved his greatest business success. It might be called Trump USA, for it appears that he is at work on turning the Presidency into the greatest money-making venture of all time. In an apparent Freudian slip during a joint news conference with Angela Merkel a couple of months after inauguration; Trump gave an ominous hint of his view of America and his Presidency.

"The United States has been treated very, very unfairly by many countries over the years and that's going to stop. We're a very powerful company... country." [13]

In a brilliant move, he stated that he will not accept his salary as President. But, this is peanuts compared to where the real money is. His Florida resort, Mar-a-Lago, is one money maker; but it is by no means the only one. Through Dec 11, 2017, he had been at one of his private clubs at least 98 days since assuming the Presidency. (An update – Add nine days to the above through Dec 31, 2017; since he was at Mar-a-Lago from Dec 22, 2017 through the end of the year)[14] So what's the big deal? Obama and previous Presidents had spent a lot of time

golfing. The difference is that the money spent by Secret Service, reporters, and fellow golfers was not going into the President's coffers.

Members at his various golf clubs include dozens of lobbyists, trade union officials, and CEO's of companies holding government contracts. And, membership does not come cheap at any of the clubs with thousands more in annual dues. According to financial disclosure documents, the take amounted to about $600 million in 2015 and 2016.[15] Mar-a-Lago membership doubled to $200,000 in January 2017.[16] With fees going up since Trump became President, one can only imagine what the take will be in 2018 and beyond.

In addition to a number of golf resorts, the Trump organization owns a vast array of hotels and other properties domestically and abroad. One of these is the Trump International Hotel, just blocks from the White House; and through August 11, 2017 $1.97 million profit since the beginning of the year.[17] Rates run $650 a night or about $150 more than comparable hotels in the area. At least his competitors can't accuse him of undercutting the market. But his hotel has one advantage that the others don't; and that is the opportunity to mingle with the President and high staff. Although the hotel is not recording high occupancy rates; the clientele regularly includes high ranking foreign dignitaries.[18]

Interestingly, the Embassy of Kuwait moved their annual celebration of independence which had been held at the Washington Four Seasons for several years to Trump International in February 2017.[19]

Even more suspect are a number of his international venues with respect to conflicts of interest in foreign policy. Trump's executive order, banning nationals from seven countries entry into the United States under the guise of threatened terrorism is very interesting. The counties affected (Iran, Iraq, Libya,

Somalia, Sudan, Syria, and Yemen) have two things in common. He has no business interests in any of those countries; and there have been no lethal attacks in the U.S. for at least twenty years by Muslim extremists from any of those countries.[20]

On the other hand, the nineteen terrorists involved in the September 11, 2001 attacks, were from Muslim counties that were exempted from the ban. Interestingly, all four of those counties (Saudi Arabia, Egypt, Lebanon, and the United Arab Emirates) had another thing in common. Can you guess? I'll bet you got it. Trump has business operations in each of them.[21]

But please remember, Donald is not taking his annual salary of $400,000.

Chapter 4 Inferiority Complex

"Mirror, mirror on the wall; who is the fairest one of all?"

Donald has certainly started out the new year (2018) with a bang. Here are his latest quotes, apparently triggered by Wolfe's just published book, *Fire and Fury*, questioning his fitness for the Presidency. *"I am a very stable genius"*[1] and *"Actually throughout my life, my two greatest assets have been mental stability and being like, really smart."*[2] One needn't be a psychiatrist or have a PhD in psychology to recognize that Donald may have an ego problem. And to a great many, that assertion is a gross understatement.

"...I will tell you this in a non-braggadocios way... there has never been a 10-month president that has accomplished what we have accomplished. That I can tell you. That I can tell you... And the numbers going up are going to do much better than anybody anticipates. In fact, they're going to say that Trump is the opposite of an exaggerator – the exact opposite... They're going to start saying . that he <Trump> ought to be a little bit more optimistic because his predictions were low, can you believe it? You know, a year and a half ago they were saying, oh he can't do that. Now they're saying, hmm, that was quick... And remember, I was the one when I was here the last time, I said, we're going to have Christmas again; I was the one that said you go to the department stores and you see Happy New Year and you see red and you see snow and you see all these things. You don't see Merry Christmas anymore... With Trump as your president, we are going to be celebrating Merry Christmas again, and it's going to be done with a big beautiful tax cut. Thank you everybody. God bless you. Thank you. Thank you everybody. Thank you very much." [3]

In case you haven't noticed, Donald seems to rely on certain words an awful lot. He apparently likes the words *great, greatest, best,* and *very.* His most repeated phrase, "Make America Great Again" is continually echoed by his supporters. But what's that got to do with the title of this chapter? It is simply that an individual that obsesses about himself and is always defensive to criticism is a very insecure person. He needs that continual assurance that he is important. It has been reported that Donald watches TV at least four hours a day, switching channels when he is not the main news.

If bragging was the only problem with an insecure person; it wouldn't be so bad. One could always turn him off; but a person with an inferiority complex has to prove it. He needs to prove it to himself as well as others. He does that by bullying.

Bullies like to intimidate and take advantage of people they perceive to be weaker than they, which serves to enhance their own self-worth. They want to feel superior; and they want other people to feel that they (bullies) are superior.

Trump's alleged sexual harassment of women fits the pattern. He, of course, has strenuously denied the allegations; but, interestingly for someone not unacquainted with lawsuits, has never bothered to sue for libel. At the time of this writing there are nineteen women who have alleged sexual harassment or worse.

And, as would be expected, he has not confined his bullying to sexual aggression. Donald habitually denigrates women that refuse to kowtow to him or those he considers unattractive. During the first debate of the primaries, Megyn Kelly, one of the moderators, asked him about his put down of women. She followed up, referring to his comment to a contestant on *The Celebrity Apprentice* show, that... *"it would be a pretty picture to see her on her knees. Does that sound to you like the temperament of a man we should elect as president?"*

26

He evaded the question but later in a tweet attacked Kelly as unprofessional and *"not very good."* He obviously was not very happy with Kelly's questions and later referred to her as a *"bimbo"* and *"highly overrated."*

In an interview with *Rolling Stone Magazine* after the debate Donald denigrated Carly Fiorina, one of the seventeen Republican candidates. *"Look at that face. Would anyone vote for that? Can you imagine that, the face of our next President?"*[4]

And then there was one woman, Jessica Leeds, who accused Trump of groping her on a plane. His comment, *"Look at her. She would not be my first choice."*[5]

During the campaign, he viciously mocked a disabled reporter. And then there are the small contractors and employees mentioned in the previous chapter. As mentioned, there have been numerous lawsuits, but the independent contractor generally finds himself out-gunned by Trump's lawyers, who are on retainer.

There's another thing about bullies. They are generally cowards. That is the reason they prey on those they presume are weaker. Their inferiority complex shows up very clearly when the person being bullied stands up to the bully. Typically, the bully fades away because he is really a coward. Was the bone spur really the reason for Donald's avoiding military service or was there possibly another reason?

Furthermore, Donald's alleged history of aggressive behavior toward women not only fits the pattern of an individual suffering from an inferiority complex; but that of a coward as well. One can only imagine what the outcome would be if a woman he ever accosts has training in martial arts. Of course, since he focuses on attractive females; women of his own size need have no fear.

In January 2016, one week before the Iowa caucuses and two

days before the second Republican primary debate, Trump announced that he would be boycotting the Fox News sponsored event. A few days earlier, he had hinted that he just might do that after it was announced that Megyn Kelly would again be a co-moderator. Trump tweeted that Kelly was biased and should not be a moderator. Senator Ted Cruz chastised Trump and asked if he couldn't stand up to Kelly, how could voters anticipate that he would stand up to Putin and the Ayatollah. Following a public backlash against his decision, Trump announced that he would be hosting an event to benefit Wounded Warriors on the same night as the debate. Cruz responded by challenging Trump to a one-on-one debate "any time any place" prior to the Iowa caucuses. Trump's campaign manager replied that Mr. Trump would be happy to have a one-on-one debate with Cruz if and when he was the last man standing. As it would turn out, Cruz challenged Trump twice more, once prior to the Wisconsin primary; and then again, just prior to the Indiana primary. At that point in time, the race had come down to essentially two men, Trump and Cruz; so, the condition of "last man standing" had been met. Nevertheless, there was no debate.

Finally, a coward doesn't have the courage to own up to his shame and frequently covers his cowardice by resorting to fanciful depictions of heroism. After the horrific school shooting of February 2018 in Parkland Florida where a sheriff's deputy failed to enter the school and confront the shooter; Trump said he would have run in unarmed and tackled the assailant.[6] What a hero! We can only wish that he had been there.

Chapter 5 Charity

In the previous chapter, I mentioned Donald's proclivity for boasting as a way of boosting his self-esteem; but as with his business dealings, his "philanthropy" comes into play.

An incident in 1996 exemplifies his need for self-glorification. It was a charity gala to support a new nursery school for children with AIDS. The major donors were seated up front with the mayor and former mayor of New York. Donald came in and took the reserved seat of another donor who arrived late. As it turns out, he was not a major donor or even a donor at all. But the program had started and no one said a word. As the children sang, *"This Little Light of Mine,"* in front of the group of donors and Trump; a photographer was snapping pictures with Donald smiling and looking for all the world like he was one of the honored benefactors. When the program was over, Trump left without a word or a donation.[1]

After the devastation of Hurricane Harvey in 2017, President Trump made a trip to Texas and announced that he would be making a big donation with his *"own money"*.

Mr. President, I am sure the victims of Hurricane Harvey as well as people around the country are appreciative of your generosity; but just a word of respectful advice. You might open your Bible and see what Jesus Christ had to say about publicizing charity. In case you are a little bit rusty, permit me to refresh your memory: Matthew 6: 1-4. If that's too much of a hassle, how about checking with some of your evangelical supporters who think you are so great?

You might also ask your Jewish daughter and son-in law to explain tsedakah, the Hebrew word for charity.

Since Jesus was a Jew, there is no conflict. Tsedakah should be given anonymously and at least without fanfare. But of course, classy people of all faiths already know that instinctively.

By the way, although you haven't mentioned it; I'm sure you will also want to make a large donation with 'your own money' to the victims of Hurricane Irma in Puerto Rico and the Virgin Islands.

After I had posted the above open letter to Trump on Face Book, I received the usual ad hominem attacks; but the reply that brought me laughing to tears was the one that read, *"President Trump has given so much to charity over the years anonymously that nobody has heard anything about."*

I replied, *"And all this time I had accused the President of trying to hide some shenanigans by not making his tax returns public; when he was just trying to keep all those charitable contributions anonymous."* I never heard back from that dear lady; but I suspect that she was happy with my apparent "apology".

Charity is not a term that jumps to mind when discussing Trump; but I thought it might be worthwhile to look at some examples of his philanthropy. As with many wealthy people, Donald has a charitable foundation, which can be a very good thing. An individual is allowed to make tax deductible donations to one's own foundation, which can then disburse the funds as a Board of Directors sees fit. All fine and good so long as the disbursal is to a bonafide charity with no ties to the individual.

Unfortunately, there have been some alleged irregularities that have not been cleared up to the satisfaction of New York state's attorney general.[2]

In chapter 2, we discussed Donald's fondness of leverage. Obviously, he doesn't believe in restricting its use to business. At a campaign stop in Kenansville, North Carolina in September 2016, after a report came out that he had used over $250,000 in foundation funds for some litigation involving his business interests, he actually

bragged that "...*there's nothing like doing things with other people's money. Because it takes the risk – you get a good chunk out of it and it takes the risk.*"

Since the foundation's inception in 1988, initially funded from proceeds of the book, *The Art of the Deal,* through 2015, Donald had contributed $5.5 million to the Trump Foundation while outside donors contributed an additional $9.3 million.[3] Since making a $35,000 gift in 2008, he has made no additional personal donations to the foundation.[4]

Following are some other questionable charitable contributions: The list is certainly not comprehensive.

1. In 2007, Melania Trump bid $20,000 at a charity art auction held at Mar-a-Lago to purchase a six-foot painting of her husband using foundation funds.[5]

2. Donald obviously likes the subject; since he purchased a four-foot painting of himself for another $20,000 at a charity event in 2014, again held at Mar-a-Lago. Needless to say, but this too was with foundation money.[6]

3. In 2012, Donald, bid $12,000 in foundation money to win a football helmet signed by quarterback Tim Tebow and football jersey.[7]

4. And then, leave it to the intrepid entrepreneur to pull this one off. Donald "donated" $150,000 of another foundation's money to a police group that then paid more than $200,000 for its gala on Trump's property. It's unclear how much of that $200,000 was profit; but since Trump was not out of pocket for the donation, he came out richer. To top it off he received an award for his philanthropy; because the group didn't know it wasn't Trump's own money.[8]

5. In a smaller example of the same type of deal, the German-American Hall of Fame, rented space at Trump Tower for about $20,000. Donald followed up with a gift of $1,000 from the Trump Foundation.[9]

6. Trump Foundation's $264,631 — was used to renovate a fountain outside the windows of Trump's Plaza Hotel.[10]

7. In 2008, at a gala hosted by Gucci to benefit Madonna's charity, Donald bid more than $100,000 for a trip to Paris, earning him press from New York to London. But, again, it was with money from his foundation to which he had donated just $30,000 that year. It is unknown who, if anyone got the benefit of the trip.[11]

8. On September 17, 2013, there was a $25,000 foundation donation to a group supporting Pam Bondi's campaign. Interestingly, just a four days earlier than when she received the check she announced that she was deliberating joining New York attorney general's fraud suit against Trump University. Shortly thereafter Bondi decided not to pursue the case for lack of evidence.[12] Of course, the timing was mere coincidence; since Bondi insists that there was no connection. Now, as this is being written in December 2017, Bondi is saying that Mueller's investigation into possible Russian collusion by Trump's campaign staff should be dropped.[13]

9. In 2014, there was a foundation donation of $100,000 to Citizens United – a conservative political activist group.[14] The size of that donation and the type of organization rather than a typical charitable organization might cause one to wonder about Trump's interest. It turns out that Citizen's United was involved in a lawsuit against New York's Attorney General who was suing Trump for fraud in the Trump University case. I suppose we are to believe that is just another interesting coincidence.

As revealing as the above uses of foundation money are, I think we need to take a look at some other anecdotal evidence outside the realm of foundation assets to get a fuller perspective of how Donald views charity in general.

In an August 2015 campaign debate, he was asked about an interview he had in July where he acknowledged donating to Hillary Clinton in her 2008 campaign for senator and said, *"When you give, they do whatever the hell you want them to do." "You'd better believe it,"* Trump said. *"If I ask them, if I need them, you know, .."*

"You know what? When I need something from them, two years later, three years later, I call them, and they are there for me. . . . ." He went on to say that *"it's a broken system."*[15] Indeed it is; and the sad part is that there are some who believe Trump is the one to fix it.

In other words, he apparently doesn't give anything without expecting something back. Granted, the context wasn't about giving to charity; but as we've seen, he doesn't seem to have any compunction about using charity money for his own purposes.

In the next section I will cover promises; but since the following fall under charity, I chose to discuss these here. During the campaign, Trump had made three promises to allay thoughts that this wealthy businessman might be seeking office to feather his nest. Perish the thought. The Presidential salary of $400,000 was unimportant to him. He would decline to take it and let the Treasury keep it since they needed it a lot more than he did.

It appears that he has done so; at least for 2017. But the other two promises are far more significant in money value and also inability to track.

He promised that the inauguration celebration would be a no frills affair; and any excess of the record setting $90 million inauguration fund over actual inauguration costs would be donated to charity. There were no details as to any public accounting; and to date, we are still waiting for that accounting. Perhaps, we will get the public accounting when we get to see Trump's tax returns.

The other promise was that any profits earned from any foreign governments' use of his hotel rooms and banquet space would be donated to the U.S. treasury.[16] Again, there have been no details as to how the public would be able to verify that any donation would accurately reflect profit was given.

But, there was one promise with respect to lodging that I wish he had made, but didn't. Melania and Baron will continue to live at Trump Tower in New York while school is in session. This means that the Secret Service will have to look out for the two; and by necessity, will be staying (and paying) at Trump Tower. Furthermore, every trip that Donald makes to Mar-a-Lago or another of his clubs or hotels will require Secret Service personnel to stay as well. It would have been nice for him to say that all charges to Secret Service at his venues would be complimentary.

There have also been the promises to donate to charity all profits from a number of his business ventures. In addition to the aforementioned *The Art of the Deal,* are

Trump Vodka, Trump University, *Trump-The Game,* and his latest book, *Crippled America* that he has pledged all profits to charity. With the exception of *The Art of the Deal,* the only accounting of contributions for the latter business ventures showed a few hundred dollar donation from Trump Vodka profits to a group supporting Walter Reed Hospital. [17]

On the ill-fated Trump University, profits of which, Trump had pledged to charity; he told a group in South Carolina that he would have given all the money to charity, *"had he not been sued".*[18]

Apparently, we shouldn't blame Trump; rather, the

ungrateful students that chose to sue him.

Chapter 6 Racism

"I am not a racist...I am the least racist person you will interview; that I can tell you." Donald said this in an interview with CNN after the firestorm created by his alleged remarks during the January 11, 2018 bi-partisan meeting on immigration at the White House. Senator Durbin reported that the President had referred to Haiti and African countries as *"shit-hole countries"* that we don't need more immigrants from; and that we need to send them back. He said further we need more Norwegians that can contribute to our country. The implication was clear although denied by Trump and his cult that white people were desirable and people of color not.

It wasn't a day later that Donald was denying the reported profane remarks; but acknowledging that he had used *"strong language"*. Despite the denial, much of his cult were defending the remarks as true. I had posted the following on FaceBook and got a barrage of inflammatory and ad hominem responses from his cult:

"Congratulations to you Trump supporters for being in fine company with David Duke and his followers as you all cheered the remarks that Trump denied uttering."

A few of the more polite responses actually praised him for the *'shit-hole'* remark, saying they agreed with him in describing those countries and that's exactly why they voted for him in *'calling a spade a spade'*. I find that just a touch ironic with as often as their man changes positions.

But be that as it may, when I pointed out that the profanity describing those countries was not the most offensive thing he said in that meeting; but rather denigrating the people. He said that we don't need more of those people. What we need are more Norwegians. That elicited more ad hominems; but one respondent was honest enough to agree with that part of his statement as well; but somehow didn't see it as racist.

Let's look back on his history of race relations and see if we can gain a bit more perspective.

1. In the seventies, Trump gave preferential treatment to whites while attempting to deny renting to blacks.[1]

2. There was discriminatory behavior to black employees at his casinos.[2]

3. He urged the death penalty for the five black and Latin teens accused of raping a white woman in Central Park in 1989. During the campaign in 2016 Trump was still insisting they were guilty ten years after DNA evidence had proved them innocent.[3]

4. Trump began his campaign in 2016 with a speech referring to Mexican immigrants as criminals and rapists.[4]

5. In December 2015, he proposed a complete ban on Muslims entering the U.S., including American citizens who were out of the country.[5]

6. He tried to get a judge removed from his Trump University lawsuit, arguing that the judge couldn't be fair because of his Mexican heritage.[6]

7. He had far harsher words for his fellow Republican candidates in the 2016 Presidential campaign than for David Duke. When pressed after first saying he didn't know anything about him, he finally "*disavowed*' him and his followers. [7]

8. Further, on February 1, 2017, Trump asked the Director of Homeland Security to change the name and focus of

the program, which heretofore had been known as *'Countering Violent Extremism'* to *'Countering Islamic Extremism'*. It would no longer target such groups as white supremacists, who have also carried out bombings and shootings in the U.S.[8]

I, of course, can't read Donald's mind. He may, indeed, not see himself as a racist. His perception of himself would certainly be in line with his other apparent self-delusions. But with that being said, despite Donald's protests, as the old saying goes; *"if it looks like a duck, walks like a duck, and quacks like a duck, it may just be a duck."* However, giving him the benefit of the doubt; if he is no racist, and only acts like a racist; *what difference does it make?*

Part II Promises

Chapter 7 Promises, promises

Every politician makes promises; and it isn't rare for a politician to break one. A famous one that cost the President re-election, was George H.W. Bush's *"Read my lips."* However, most politicians refrain from making too many promises for fear of having to answer for broken ones. But that concern apparently doesn't bother Trump. He surely holds the record for promises broken; he may even have achieved the record for promises issued.

By one count, he had made 663 promises[1] during his campaign. Most were inconsequential or humorous like his promise to never participate in a bicycle race after Senator Kerry had broken a leg, or to drop that *"dirty, rotten traitor"* Bowe Bergdahl out of an airplane without a parachute. He also promised to not kill journalists, just because he *"hate<s> some of them...";* and to never address Iran's leader by his preferred title, the Supreme Leader. Further, if he were to be elected President; we would all be saying, *"Merry Christmas"* again. One promise we can probably count on is that he would be unpredictable. Trump also promised not to make any crazy comments as president. *"...I will be so presidential that you won't even recognize me. You'll be falling asleep,* you'll be so bored."

Many others were so nebulous that there would be no way to keep him accountable; or show that he had anything to do with it. Still others are of little consequence except to his base like ," *...frequently use the term 'radical Islamic terrorism'."*

But, here are some of his more pertinent broken promises:

1. *Eliminate Common Core – it's "a disaster" and "very*

bad thing. Might even eliminate the Department of Education.[2] Status – Trump may not have realized that his promise conflicts with the Tenth Amendment. Common Core is a state's prerogative, and as of June 2017, 39 states were using it or a modification.[3] As for doing away with the Department of Education, there has been no indication of anything underway.

2. *EPA might also disappear.*[4] Too nebulous to evaluate. Lots of things might happen in the future; but there is no indication that EPA will fade into history.

3. *Rebuild the country's aging infrastructure at one-third of what U.S. is currently paying for such projects.* [5] Infrastructure spending is on the agenda for 2018. It's going to be rough going with deficit hawks fighting and individual interests campaigning for their own piece of the pie. As for Trump's cost estimate; it strikes one as typical bluster with no substance.

4. *Defund Planned Parenthood.*[6] When??

5. *Never take a vacation while serving as president.*[7] That one is laughable. It probably deserves to be under lies; but since it is impossible to read his mind in retrograde, I'll give him the benefit of the doubt and just call it a *"huge"* broken promise.

6. *Cut the budget by 20 percent by simply renegotiating.*[8] When?? As is so typical, Trump makes a statement with nothing to back it up. With his plans for infrastructure spending, it's probably safe to say that there is little likelihood of any budget cuts for the foreseeable future.

7. *Reduce the $18 trillion national debt.*[9] When?? Refer to #6 above.

8. *"We'll put our people back to work, we will not let other countries steal our jobs. It is not going to happen*

anymore." [10] As of December 1, 2017, 93,000 American jobs had been lost since Trump's election.[11]

9. *"I'm going to instruct my Treasury Secretary to label China, and I like China, they're my tenant, they buy condos all the time, they're just fine, but you know what, they're a currency manipulator and we're going to apply tariffs to any country that devalues its currency to gain an unfair advantage over the United States."* [12] In April 2017 Trump announced that he would not follow through with that promise; since ostensibly, China is no longer devaluing their currency.[13] Unfortunately, that is only half true. China is not intentionally devaluing their currency; but the effect is the same. China's economy is slowing, resulting in a currency decline.[14]

10. *"So the first priority of my administration will be to preserve and protect our religious liberty. The First Amendment guarantees our right to practice our faith as we see fit, not just during the holy days, but all the time, always, wherever."*[15] This promise, obviously, hasn't extended to Islam as will be discussed in the chapter on immigration.

11. *"Policy decisions will be public and very, very transparent. They won't be made on Hillary's private email account."*[16] Donald loves superlatives. If his first year in office is any indication of how the rest of the term may go with respect to transparency, his administration may go down as one of the *most* opaque in recent history. Starting with his refusal to make public his tax returns and then refusing to divest his vast holdings gave an early glimpse into how well that promise was going to be kept. Donald may think that his activity on Twitter constitutes transparency; and indeed, it does show us something, but it is something most of us knew already. Namely, that Donald is a self-absorbed egotist. That is intentionally

understated to avoid a possible defamation lawsuit. As the year progressed, our early hint of the secretive nature of this administration was confirmed by the lack of forthrightness on the administration's key personnel dealings with Russia.

12. *Diplomatic appointments will be made to great negotiators, "not nice people that got there by political donations."*[17] Terry Bronstad, former Iowa Governor, with no previous international diplomatic experience and whose backing was responsible for Trump's strong second place finish in Iowa's primary caucus and also his win in the general election was appointed ambassador to China,.

13. Woody Johnson, owner of the New York Jets and large political donor to Trump was appointed to become ambassador to the UK. He also had no previous diplomatic experience.

14. *"But one thing I can promise you is this: I will always tell you the truth."*[18] And, I'll bet his cult believes him. See the next section.

15. *"If I win, day one, we are going to announce our plans to renegotiate NAFTA."*[19] As this is being written in January 2018, we're still awaiting the plan.

16. *Will propose "on day one...a constitutional amendment to impose term limits on all members of congress"*[20] We're still waiting; but, even if he does, it will be meaningless. Congress will not support it and neither will state legislators aspiring to Congress.

17. *Strengthen the military so that it's "so big and so strong and so great" that "nobody's going to mess with us."*[21] Too nebulous. Besides, funding is going to be a big problem. .

18. *"Bomb the s--- out of ISIS." Also bomb oil fields controlled by the Islamic State, then seize the oil and give the profits to military veterans who were wounded while fighting."*[22] Seize the oil?? How about returning it to the previous owners before ISIS seized it? Donald, you've shown how much you love veterans; but how about for a change using some of your own money instead of what you refer to as OPM?

19. *Target and kill the relatives of terrorists.*[23] His base would love this; but it will never happen. Congress and the military would resist and hopefully, some of his advisors would stand up to him on this, If we were to do it; we would become an international pariah. And, there would be the threat of trial for war crimes at some future date.

20. *Shut down parts of the Internet so that Islamic State terrorists cannot use it to recruit American children.*[24] How?? Too nebulous, and Donald is just blowing hot air.

21. *Bring back waterboarding, which the Obama administration considers torture. Trump has said he's willing to use interrogation techniques that go even further than waterboarding. Even if such tactics don't work, "they deserve it anyway, for what they're doing."*[25] The overwhelming consensus of intelligence experts is that such methods do not work; and, furthermore are counter-productive. Again, we would outrage the international community; and there could be grounds for conviction of war crimes in the future.

22. *Will not settle the Trump University lawsuit.*[26] In November, Trump agreed to settle the case for $25 million.[27]

I realize that the students of Trump University feel cheated; but they did come away with one valuable business lesson. Be careful who you do business with.

Chapter 8 Hillary

The calls for *"Lock her up."* had almost become the campaign slogan displacing *"Make America Great Again"*. Donald had smiled when hearing the phrase; but before the second Presidential debate had not expressed that himself. However, Donald was apparently triggered by taking some heat about his saucy Billy Bush video and decided to do some diversion. *"And I tell you what, I didn't think I would say this, but I'm going to and I hate to say it. But if I win, I am going to instruct my attorney general to get a special prosecutor to look into your situation. Because there has never been so many lies, so much deception. There has never been anything like it. And we're gonna have a special prosecutor. When I speak, I go out and speak, the people of this country are furious. In my opinion, the people that have been long time workers at the FBI are furious. There has never been anything like this where e-mails, and you get a subpoena. You get a subpoena, and after getting the subpoena you delete 33,000 e-mails and then you acid wash them or bleach them, as you would say. Very expensive process. So we're gonna get a special prosecutor and we're gonna look into it. Because you know what, people have been − their lives have been destroyed for doing 1/5 of what you have done. And it's a disgrace, and honestly, you oughta be ashamed of yourself. . . ."* [1]

But a couple of months later, right after winning the election; he must have had a change of heart. He told Jeff Sessions, his Attorney General to be, to not pursue an indictment since *"I don't want to hurt the Clintons, I really don't. She went through a lot and suffered greatly in many different ways."* [2]

It's no secret that Donald and the Clintons have been close

friends for years. Donald recently acknowledged backing Hillary in her run for the Senate in 2008; but said that was all politics, since New York was a Democratic state.

And, it also well known that Donald and Bill Clinton had a friendly chat a day or two before Trump announced his candidacy. It was speculated that Bill encouraged his good friend to run. We will never know; but it makes sense in that Clinton knew that Trump would be a divisive force in the Republican Party and make it that much easier for Hillary to win. Was Trump complicit in that thinking, at least before it appeared he could actually win the nomination? Again, we'll never know.

Then all of a sudden, six months into his term, Donald apparently had another change of heart; or at least forgot what he had told Sessions right after the election. He started complaining that his AG was not going after Hillary for all those classified e-mails that she had deleted.[3]

Although Sessions probably prudently did not ask his boss why the change of heart; many others of us wonder if there had been a new batch of incriminating e-mails or other evidence against Hillary that was found. Or, just possibly, that the Russia collusion investigation was getting a little too close; and a diversion was necessary?

Chapter 9 Taxes

"I know our complex tax laws better than anyone who has ever run for president and am the only one who can fix them." This was a tweet by the President on October 2, 2016. This came right after a story in the New York Times revealing that Trump had declared a 916 million dollar loss in 1995 that would result in his having a zero tax liability for a number of years.[1] Trump acknowledged that the story was true; and that he had merely taken legal advantage of a tax code that was terribly unfair due to all the loopholes. His message in a nut shell: *"Just elect me and I will fix it."*

So now we are looking at what he promised. *Lo and behold*, the widely ballyhooed bill now known as *The Tax Cut and Jobs Act of 2017* was actually passed and signed into law on December 22, 2017. Maybe, I'm missing something; but I don't see that any loopholes have been eliminated or much of anything that I would term *reform*. Generally, the word implies making changes to something to improve it; but I guess another definition of reform could refer to changing anything, whether or not it was for the better. Maybe, that's why the new law is not referred to as *The Tax Reform Act of 2017*. But, perhaps, I am being too harsh.

During a campaign stop in Gettysburg Pennsylvania on October 22, 2016, Donald declared that a *"middle class family with two children will get basically, approximately, a 35% tax cut."*[2] Really? *"basically approximately"*. That's impressive.

So, what is a middle class family? If you lived in the hills of eastern Tennessee or out in the country in New Mexico; I suppose you could get along quite well on an income that would classify as poverty in Manhattan or San Francisco. The Pew

Research Center calculated that the American middle class income ranged from $42,000 to $125,000 in 2014. That's quite a range, so let's just take the average, round up to $85,000, and say that the income is all salary for simplification.

If you were in that median income four person family group with itemized deductions of $24,000, which I will designate Family A, congratulations! Your family was one of the U.S.Treasury lottery winners. Not quite 35%, but 21.2% isn't bad. (See appendix for calculations.) If your family income was less than $85,000 and/or your itemized deductions were less than $24,000, you came out better. And, if you have three or more children, you made out like a bandit.

However, as with all lotteries, there are losers as well as winners. If your family is an "empty nester" with the same income and itemized deductions as Family A, which we will call Family B; you barely broke even with a "gain" of 0.48%. OK. But, how about a senior couple (Family C) with the same income and inordinate medical expenses, resulting in itemized deductions of $30,000? This unfortunate family loses 2.41% under the new tax law. So, the savings have disappeared; and it is obvious that as income drops below $85,000, coupled with increasing itemized deductions, the situation will get worse for a family with no children as a result of the new tax law.

Two other consequences of the new law should be mentioned. The first is a real irony for the party of supposed fiscal responsibility. The non-partisan CBO estimates that the new law will result in trillion dollar deficits over the next ten years.[3] The second results in a real boon for the mega-rich due to the death tax revision and the 'pass through' provision,

Some reform, huh? Maybe, Donald and the Republicans will be lucky and not have too many of their supporters that fall into family category C.

Chapter 10 Immigration

Immigration is one subject that, apparently, is near and dear to his heart, as it is to his minions. Just lately, he reportedly made an interesting comment that brought on a firestorm. Donald denied making the exact remark; but acknowledged talking *"rough"*. It occurred (or didn't occur) on January 11, 2018, the second day of a bi-partisan meeting at the White House, to try to achieve a consensus on immigration, which involved a number of key issues. Among them were *DACA (deferred action on children); CHIP (children's health insurance program);* the eleven million illegal immigrants currently living in the U.S.; reform of current immigration policy; and the *Wall*.

A day prior to the alleged inflammatory remark, Donald appeared ready to deal. *"I think my positions are going to be what the people in the room come up with. If they come to me with things I'm not in love with, I'm going to do it. <sign the bill> Because I respect them."* [1]

Apparently, Donald had a radical change of heart overnight that just maybe was influenced a bit by certain Republican hard-liners. Some suspect, however, that what he said the second day actually reflected his own beliefs on the matter, given his leanings on race, discussed in a previous chapter.

Senator Durbin stated that Trump had used vile language, referring to African countries as *"shit-hole countries"* and had said that *"Those shit-holes send us the people they don't want."* asked *"why America would want to accept more immigration from Haiti?"* when Senator Graham had mentioned Haitians that had fled here from the ravages of hurricanes as being in a temporarily protected category. Trump also reportedly said to *"put me down for more Europeans to come to this country. Why can't we get more people from Norway?"* [2]

Donald, a day later, denied using those words; and two Republican Senators as well as the Secretary of DHS said they didn't recall hearing those words. Senator Graham, however, did not dispute Senator Durbin's recollection.

Among his campaign promises regarding immigration were to:

1. Deport the almost 11 million immigrants illegally living in the United States.[3]

2. End birthright citizenship.[4]

3. Temporarily ban most foreign Muslims from entering the United States with exceptions for dignitaries, business people, athletes and others who have "proven" themselves *"until <we> can figure out what is going on."* [5] This morphed into a *"total and complete"* ban on Muslims entering the U.S. on December 7, 2016. When asked if that included Muslim Americans currently out of the country; Trump's reply was *"all Muslims".* [6]

4. Bar Syrian refugees from entering the country and kick out any who are already living here.[7] This is one campaign promise that Trump partially fulfilled after becoming President. His executive order of January 27, 2017, denies admission of Syrian refugees indefinitely and also bars admission from seven Muslim countries for ninety days. I already discussed some notable exceptions to his Muslim country ban in chapter 4. An interesting consequence of his Syria ban is that it includes Christians who are citizens of Syria. There is no need to worry, however; since his ban was overturned by Federal court.

5. Create a database of Syrian refugees. Trump hasn't ruled out creating a database of Muslims in the country. [8]

6. Heavily surveil mosques in the United States. Trump has said he's open to the idea of closing some mosques.[9]

7. Triple the number of U.S. Immigration and Customs Enforcement officers.[10]

8. *Continue to allow lowly paid foreign workers to come to the United States on temporary works visas because "they are the only ones who want to pick grapes."*[11]

9. I thought this was one of Trump's facetious remarks until I found out that Trump Winery in Charlottesville VA this year Jan 2018 had applied for special work permits for foreign workers since they couldn't find Americans to work for $10.72/hr.

Chapter 11 Climate Change
and Global Warming

Throughout Trump's campaign he had been dismissive of anthropogenic global warming and climate change, continually referring to them as a hoax. Back in 2012, he had tweeted that the *"concept of global warming was created by and for the Chinese to make U.S. manufacturing less competitive."*[1] Nevertheless, Donald has shown through subsequent remarks and energy policies to have little understanding or interest in understanding climate science.

While those of us who are of the opinion that the *theory* of global warming and climate change is flawed; and are happy to see some of Obama's climate change policies rolled back, Donald's ignorance lessens our credibility. Specifically, his comments regarding the Paris Accords and his support for corn-based ethanol as a gasoline extender belie his understanding of the science.

Donald, as promised, backed out of the Paris Accords; but he showed his lack of understanding by leaving the door open to renegotiate. His idea was that the Accords were punitive to the U.S., and that the CO_2 restrictions should be eased. What he should have said is that the U.S. has no interest in an agreement based on pseudo-science that would cost not only our country but the rest of the world an exorbitant amount of money and resources. Our scientists will be happy to share their findings so that the countries of the world can devote their resources to address real problems like hunger and disease.

There is zero scientific or economic basis for requiring gasoline to be extended with corn-based ethanol. The flawed idea behind it is that burning ethanol releases less CO_2 than gasoline, which on a gallon for gallon or pound for pound is true. But that does not take into account the difference in energy between equivalent weights of the two, nor the cost of production.

There is another irony that is often overlooked and that is in preparing a suitable low moisture ethanol, distillation is required. This step would normally require a heat source, that depending on the fuel would contribute additional CO_2. The rational conclusion is that if the whole idea is political (which it appears to be), continue to subsidize corn; but instead of using it to make ethanol to extend gasoline, just use the whole corn plant as an extender in a coal fired utility. But that's probably too deep for Donald.

Chapter 12 The Wall

One of Trump's big promises was to **"build a wall along the southern border that's taller than the arenas where Trump holds his rallies, taller than any ladder and one foot taller than the Great Wall of China. This artistically beautiful wall will be constructed out of hardened concrete, rebar and steel, and it will be the greatest wall that you've ever seen – so great that the nation will likely one day name it 'The Trump Wall'.**[1]

And then at a Phoenix, Arizona campaign speech on August 31, 2016, Trump promised *"...Mexico will pay for the wall. Believe me. Hundred percent. They don't know it yet, but they're going to pay for the wall... On day one we will begin working on an impenetrable, physical, tall, powerful, beautiful southern border wall. We will use the best technology, including above and below ground sensors...<for> the tunnels... Towers, aerial surveillance and manpower to supplement the wall, find and dislocate tunnels and keep out criminal cartels and Mexico... will work with us. I really believe it. Mexico will work with us."*[2]

I'm not sure about the rest of it; but Donald did get one thing right. Mexico doesn't know it yet. Here was the Mexican President's response. *"Mexico does not believe in walls... Mexico will not pay for any wall."*[3]

Donald followed up with a phone call to Peña Nieto on January 27, seven days after inauguration, ostensibly to discuss trade and immigration; but it was clear what was foremost on his mind.

"You cannot say that<Mexico will not pay for the wall.> to the press. The press is going to go with that and I cannot live

with that. You cannot say that to the press because I cannot negotiate under those circumstances." 4

So, Donald, what is there to negotiate? You said that Mexico will pay 100% of the cost of the wall. Are you thinking about offering Mexico terms, like maybe long term financing? Or maybe it will be the tariff rate on imported goods from Mexico? But what if Mexico decides to retaliate by imposing a tariff on our exports into their country? Come to think about it, maybe there is a fair amount to negotiate.

General John Kelly, who is Donald's chief of staff made an interesting and embarrassing comment about his boss and the wall on January 17, 2018; almost one year from inauguration. Trump was *"not fully informed"* when he made the promise about the wall. Kelly in a conversation with the Hispanic Congressional Caucus said that he had convinced the President that a wall wasn't necessary and that Trump's ideas had *"evolved"*.

Donald might have been well advised to listen to the General and have a ready excuse to do a little backing up. But, no; apparently Donald's feelings were hurt as he responded on his Twitter the following day: *"The Wall is the Wall; it has never changed or evolved from the first day I conceived of it."* But, *"...of necessity... never intended to be built in areas where there is natural protection such as mountains, wastelands, or tough rivers, or water..." 5*

Somehow, that doesn't sound like the great wall described at the beginning of this chapter. But that's OK, I'm sure, with his minions. They knew all along what he meant.

Chapter 13 ObamaCare

Get rid of Obamacare and replace it with something *"terrific"* that is *"so much better, so much better, so much better." Knock down the regulatory walls between states for health insurance, making plans available nationally instead of regionally."* [1]

"Repeal and replace" along with *The Wall* and deporting the eleven million illegal immigrants was a hallmark of Donald's campaign. His promise to get after it *"on Day One"* was admittedly (if not from him or any of his cult) a bit of hyperbole; but here it is one year into his term with nothing done unless one counts an element of the *Tax Cut and Jobs Act*, which eliminates the mandate, but doesn't go into effect until 2019.

Is it harsh to assign the blame on the President? After all he has had the benefit of Republican control of the House and Senate. The problem, I think, is summed up very well by Senate Majority Leader McConnell; and while he was referring to immigration, it certainly appears to fit the pattern, no matter what the issue is. *"As soon as we figure out what he is for, then I would be convinced that we were not just spinning our wheels..."* [2] What an indictment of the master of the art of the deal and supposed leader. This is the razzle dazzle quarterback wanting his team to run a play without specifying the play.

I guess the Senator is saying, *"What, Mr. President, is 'so much better'? Just give us a clue. Surely, it's not the single payer health system that you mentioned during the campaign? And do you really think Australia's socialist health system is superior to ours?*

Here's an idea. How about a full repeal of Obama Care and turn it over to the states as per the Tenth Amendment?

Chapter 14 Drain the Swamp

Another of the slogans used by the Trump campaign was to *"Drain the Swamp."* The logic was that it would take an outsider, and particularly a wealthy outsider, not beholden to special interests to shake up and clean out the corrupt establishment.

"Under my contract with the American voter we're proposing a series of ethics reforms on day one to end government – right? To end government corruption." [1]

At a campaign stop in Gettysburg, Pennsylvania on October 22, 2016, Donald stated that he would *"...work with Congress to introduce the following broader legislative measures and fight for their passage within the first 100 days of my administration.... Clean Up Corruption in Washington Act, <which> enacts tough new ethics reforms to reduce the corrupting influence of special interests, and donors, on our politics."*

OK. One day or one hundred days, no problem. After all, with all those swamp creatures swimming around in Washington; it's only understandable that it will take some time to clean things up. So here we are in the second week of February 2018 as this is written; and let's take a look at what progress has been made.

We've already covered the countless abuses of Donald's charitable foundation as well as his bragging about political donations in exchange for political favors, which by any dictionary definition, would be called bribes. There are also his vast international holdings that at the very least could compromise his handling of foreign affairs; since he has refused to divest himself and his family of potential conflicts of interest.

His refusal also to show his tax returns leave a lot of disturbing questions along those lines. And then there is the nepotism that he has shown with his daughter, Ivanka, in a key advisory position; and son-in-law, Jared Kushner, in a diplomatic role in the Middle East. Granted, they are unpaid, but still in a position to influence some personal enriching policy. Jared, by the way, failed to disclose financial ties to George Soros[2] and at least one billion dollars in loans[3] from various lenders in his security clearance application. His submitted financial statements have been revised several times;[4] and he and Ivanka still lack final security clearance, yet have had access to highly sensitive government documents.

But let's move on to the established corruption; which in promising to drain the swamp, Trump had pledged to get rid of. The one big area where he could have had a significant effect is lobbying; but by any objective measure he failed miserably. He made a big show with his executive order that banned officials from lobbying the agency they worked in for five years; but did nothing to prevent them from lobbying other government agencies.

Now, let's take a look at some of his appointees that have shown some ethical lapses or at least lack of good judgment:

1. Steven Mnuchin, Secretary of the Treasury – investment banker and CEO of One West Bank, whose firm had the unsavory reputation of rushing evictions to foreclose on underwater home owners following the housing bubble collapse. A memo from the California Attorney General's office detailed a number of "*dubious and illegal practices*" used to dispossess homeowners.[5] He sounds like someone who would fit in well in his new position of overseeing the banking industry. I'm not sure if any of that came out in his confirmation hearings, but that was history. How about some of his dealings since he has come into office? Mnuchin had requested the use of a

government plane for his honeymoon trip to Scotland, Italy, and France.[6] Thankfully, he was turned down since it would have cost taxpayers an estimated $25,000 per hour. At least, we have to give him credit for asking permission; however, on seven subsequent trips, he didn't ask permission, racking up $400,000 in tax payer expenses,[7] when he could have used commercial flights, costing less than one percent of the above. One of those flights was to Fort Knox with his bride, ostensibly to look over the gold that he is in charge of; however, it was reported that she wanted to go to see the eclipse since the view of the solar eclipse was much better in Kentucky than in Washington DC.[8]

2. Tom Price, former Secretary of Health and Human Welfare. Mr. Price, too, had a fondness for taxpayer funded air travel. He racked up a total of $1,000,000 before he was forced to resign.[9] Prior to that, in his confirmation hearings; he had faced a barrage of questions about alleged insider trading of a small Australian biotech company, and a large campaign contribution from a pharmaceutical company after he had introduced legislation as a congressman, benefitting that company.[10] Since he was confirmed; I gather that those items were not considered significant.

3. Mick Mulvaney, White House Budget Director. In his confirmation hearings, it was revealed that Mulvaney had failed to pay more than $15,000 in payroll taxes for a household employee.[11] Apparently, that was not considered an important enough offense to withhold his appointment. I guess I can see the logic. After all, if you consider his boss' history... And, maybe, we need to give this fellow some credit for holding down White House expenses. It turns out that Trump is the first President since Ulysses S. Grant, who started the tradition, of not

hosting a state dinner in the White House during his first year in office.[12] I wonder, though, if that was Mulvaney's idea, or that of his boss; since Trump probably prefers to entertain at Trump International, where his expenses would be reimbursed, and profits flow into his coffers.

4. Wilbur Ross, Secretary of Commerce. In Mr. Ross' confirmation hearings, it came out that a household employee of his was an undocumented immigrant. Of course, as soon as he found out; he fired the individual, who had worked for him seven years.[13] Again, this was not considered significant enough to withhold confirmation.

5. Scott Pruitt, Administrator of EPA. – Former Oklahoma Attorney General, self-described as *"a leading advocate against the EPA's activist agenda"* who had sued the EPA repeatedly on its actions and received major campaign contributions from the fossil fuel industry, racking in at least $215,000 between 2010 and 2014.[14] Although, I happen to agree with Pruitt and Trump on their assertion that the whole narrative of anthropogenic global warming and climate change is pseudo-science, and that EPA (as well as other Federal agencies, such as OSHA and the IRS) has become too powerful; having the fox guard the henhouse is probably not a good idea. On another issue, Pruitt has joined some of his colleagues with travel cost problems. He and his staffers had run up almost $200,000 in travel costs over six months with several first class trips to his home state on "Agency business".[15] He defended the first class travel as a security precaution. After catching a lot of heat on the above, Pruitt cancelled a trip to Israel that I assume was going to be on the taxpayers' tab.

6. Carl Icahn, former Special Advisor on Regulatory Matters-Owns a controlling interest in CVR Energy, an oil refinery that has a big problem with an EPA rule that requires refineries to mix corn-based ethanol into gasoline. The petroleum industry would much prefer that the mixing responsibility be placed on gasoline distributors. Had that rule not been in effect in 2016, CVR would have saved $205.9 million last year. [16] When this information was brought to light in August 2017, Icahn resigned.

7. Rex Tillerson, Secretary of State – Former CEO of Exxon, which has extensive interests internationally, including Russia, where the company lost one billion dollars as a result of sanctions.[17] Tillerson has reportedly divested himself of his Exxon stock; but one has to wonder about family and friends.

8. John Kelly, Chief of Staff – Retired Marine Corps General. As with all Senate confirmed nominees, General Kelly was required to list all positions held in outside organizations so that they can be vetted by the Office of Government Ethics and released to the public. He failed to disclose his board membership in two defense contractors as well as his position of vice chairman of a defense lobbying group.[18]

9. David Bernhardt, Deputy Secretary of Interior – previous employment with a lobbying firm engaged in natural resources. [19] In his current position will be overseeing the same industries he was lobbying for, very similar to Pruitt's conflicts of interest in his job.

10. Andrew F. Puzder, former nominee for Secretary of Labor – CEO of CKE Restaurants who opposes fair overtime pay as well as employee healthcare. His companies were among the fourth highest incidence of

"wage theft" reports to the government. He withdrew his nomination after this information surfaced leading to doubts that he could be confirmed.[20]

11. Michael Flynn, Former National Security Adviser-Retired Army General, charged with lying to FBI about contacts with Russians was forced to resign. Later he was indicted on illegal international finance charges and confessed in a plea deal with the Special Prosecutor as a witness in the administration's campaign collusion with Russia.[21]

The logic behind the need for an outsider to come in and clean up the corruption was certainly sound; but there are three flaws, as I see it. 1. The supposed "outsider" was anything but. He may never have previously held office; but he had been deep into politics his entire career, following in the footsteps of his father. 2. Trump, indeed, had the wealth; but his business interests had him beholden to many; and lastly, 3. Trump's history of questionable business practices would normally have made him one of the least likely to do away with similar stuff in Washington.

Rather than draining the swamp as he promised, the swamp appears murkier than ever. One Presidential historian states that the Trump Administration may well go down in history as the most corrupt ever, surpassing Warren Harding's TeaPot Dome scandal and U.S. Grant's Whiskey Ring scandal.

Part III Lies & Contradictions

"...the thing about habitual liars is that they lie habitually."

Kevin D. Williamson National Review

Poor Trump. The end of his first year and only a 35% approval rating. He must feel like Rodney Dangerfield. Just can't get any respect. He should realize that he can't please everyone, Yet, you gotta give the guy credit, He certainly tries. He reaches out to everyone; and whatever they want to hear, he is all for it. Nonetheless, all is not gloom and doom. Amazingly, he has the support of a lot of evangelicals. Money may not be able to buy happiness; but apparently it can buy support.

Chapter 15 Little lies

What is a little lie? Well, it's not as big as a big lie. Some may disagree with my designation of some of them; but to keep this book from being a multi-volume, I decided to bunch most of them here with just a sentence or two of mine as a comment.

Many of his broken promises might be categorized as lies; but that would require retrograde mind reading to the time he made the promise. I will therefore give him the benefit of the doubt and presume that he gave the promises in good faith.

IRAQ – Jan 21, 2017 *He was against going in.* Not true.[1]

VOTER FRAUD – Jan 25, 2017 *Stated that the Pew Reports confirmed.* No mention of voter fraud in the report.[2]

OBAMA'S SPEECH 2 WEEKS AGO – Jan 25, 2017 *"Two people were shot and killed during his speech.*[3] No reports of gun homicides in Chicago that day.[4]

REFUGEE VETTING – Jan 26, 2017 *"...taken in tens of thousands of people. We know nothing about them." No vetting.*[5] Untrue. Vetting lasts up to two years.[6]

COST CUTTING ON AIRPLANE – Jan 26.2017 *Trump cut "hundreds of millions of dollars on one particular plane..."* Most of the cuts had been made previously.[7]

PRESS COVERAGE – Jan 28, 2017 *NY Times and Washington Post apologized* for *false and angry coverage of Trump.* There have been no apologies from either.[8]

CUBAN AMERICAN SUPPPORT – Jan 29, 2017 *Trump got 84% of that vote.* No support of that.[9]

PRESS COVERAGE – Feb 4, 2017 *NY Times apologized for it's bad and inaccurate coverage of Trump after the election.* Again, no apologies have been made.[10]

PRESS COVERAGE OF TERRORISM – Feb 6, 2017 No press coverage of terrorism. Not true.[11]

PRESS COVERAGE – Feb 6, 2017 NY Times forced to apologize for poor reporting on Trump's win. Still, no apology.[12]

MURDER RATE – Feb 7, 2017 *Murder rate highest it's been in 47 years.* It was higher in the '80s and 90's.[13]

F-35 FIGHTER PLANE SAVINGS – Feb 7, 2017 *Trump saved more than $600 million.* The Defense Department projected that price drop before Trump took office.[14]

FLYNN'S DISCUSSION WITH RUSSIANS ON SANCTIONS – Feb 10, 2017 *Trump didn't know about it.* Yes, he did, for weeks.[15]

WALMART'S NEW JOBS – Feb 16 2017 *Wal-Mart will add 10,000 new jobs this year because of Trump's plans and initiatives* The jobs are a result of Wal-Mart's investment plans announced in October 2016.[16]

REFUGEE VETTING – Feb 18,2017 *No vetting of refugees.* Trump likes to repeat himself even when it is false. Refugees receive multiple background checks, taking up to two years. [17]

OBAMACARE COVERAGE – Feb 24, 2017 Covers very few people. Obamacare increased coverage by a net of about 20 million.[18]

CABINET APPROVAL – March 3, 2017 *Democrats still have not approved Trump's full Cabinet.* Paperwork for the last two candidates had not been submitted.[19]

WIRE TAPPING OF TRUMP'S SUITES IN TRUMP TOWER – March 4, 2017 *Obama had Trump's suites wiretapped.* The charge was fully investigated and no evidence of wiretapping was found.[20]

RELEASE OF GITMO PRISONERS – Mar 7, 2017 *122 prisoners released by Obama Administration have returned to the battlefield.* 113 of them had been released by President George W. Bush.[21]

SAVINGS ON AIRCRAFT – Mar 13, 2017 *Trump... "saved a lot of money on those jets. More than $725 million on them."* Much of the cost cuts were planned before Trump.[22]

OBAMACARE COVERAGE – Mar 13, 2017 *"...covers very few people."* About 20 million people gained insurance under ObamaCare. [23]

SAVINGS ON AIRCRAFT – Mar 15, 2017 *Trump saved $725 million.* Again, much of the cost cuts were planned before Trump.[24]

TENNESSEE INSURANCE COMPANIES – Mar 17, 2017 *Half of state has no insurance company.* There's at least one insurance company in every Tennessee county.[25]

SAVINGS ON AIRCRAFT – Mar 20, 2017 *"With just one negotiation, I saved the taxpayers... over $700 million.* Much of the cost cuts were planned before Trump.[26]

SAVINGS ON GOVERNMENT CONTRACTS – Mar 21, 2017 *"saving over $700 million on just one set of airplanes of which there are many sets."* Much of the cost cuts were planned before Trump.[27]

NATO ON TERRORISM – Mar 22, 2017 *NATO obsolete because it doesn't cover terrorism.* It has fought terrorism since the '80's.[28]

NY TIMES COVERAGE – Mar 29, 2017 *NY Times apologized after the election because it was so bad.* No, Donald. Maybe you dreamed there was an apology.[29]

NEW MICHIGAN PLANTS – March 31, 2017 *Lots of new plants going up in Michigan due to Trump's victory.* Those investments were already planned.[30]

IRAQ WAR – April 2, 2017 *Trump was totally opposed to going in.* He supported it before opposing it.[31]

TENNESSEE INSURANCE COMPANIES – April 5, 2017 *Half of state has no coverage.* There's at least one insurance company in every Tennessee marketplace.[32]

SAVINGS ON GOVERNMENT CONTRACTS – April 6, 2017 *"...look at the cost cutting we've been able to achieve with the military ...saved hundreds of millions of dollars on airplanes ...."* Much of the cost cuts were planned before Trump.[33]

STEVE BANNON'S DEPARTURE – April 11, 2017 *"...not involved in my campaign until very late... and I didn't know Steve".* Donald must have forgotten that he knew Bannon since 2011.[34]

DELAYS IN APPOINTMENTS – April 12, 2017 *Democrats obstructing appointments for hundreds of positions.* As of April 12, Trump had not nominated anyone for hundreds of positions.[35]

NATO ON TERRORISM – April 12, 2017 *NATO hadn't fought terrorism until Trump "...complained about that a long time ago; and now they do fight terrorism."* It has fought terrorism since the '80's.[36]

THE MOSUL CAMPAIGN – April 12, 2017 *"Mosul was supposed to last for a week...".* The campaign was expected to take months.[37]

TRUMP'S CHINA POSITION – April 18, 2017 *Trump hasn't changed his stance on China.* He did.[38]

SAVINGS ON AIRCRAFT – April *21, 2017 "On 90 planes I saved $725 million ...."* Much of the cost cuts were planned before Trump.[39]

HEALTH BENEFITS FOR MINERS – April 27, 2017 *Trump wants "to help our miners while the Democrats are blocking their healthcare."* The bill to extend health benefits was introduced by a Democrat and was co-sponsored by mostly Democrats.[40]

U.S. TRADE DEFICIT April 28, 2017 *U.S. has "...$17 billion trade deficit with Canada."* Nope. The U.S. had an $8.1 billion trade SURPLUS, not deficit with Canada in 2016.[41]

SAVINGS ON AIRCRAFT – April 28, 2017 *Trump saved over $725 million.* Much of the cost cuts were planned before Trump.[42]

NY TIMES COVERAGE – April 29, 2017 *Forced to apologize for covering the election so badly.* They never apologized.[43]

AIRCRAFT – April 29, 2017 *"The F-35 fighter jet program – I've saved $725 million plus, just by getting involved in the negotiation."* Much of the cost cuts were planned before Trump.[44]

CHINA CURRENCY MANIPULATION – April 29, 2017 *During the election, (due to Trump's complaining) they stopped.* China stopped years ago.[45]

OBAMACARE PRE-EXISTING CONDITIONS – May 1, 2017 *The bill will preserve coverage of pre-existing conditions.* As it stands as of May 1, it weakens coverage for pre-exiting conditions.[46]

SAVINGS ON AIRCRAFT – May 1, 2017 *"The F-35 fighter jet-I saved – I got $725 million off the price."* Much of the cost cuts were planned before Trump.[47]

SAVINGS ON AIRCRAFT – *May 2, 2017 "I love buying those planes at a reduced price...I have cut billions and billions of dollars off plane contracts sitting here."* Come on, Donald. We've been over this a dozen times. As you well know, much of the cost cuts were planned before you ever took office.[48]

U.S. TAXATION COMPARED TO REST OF WORLD – May 4, 2017 *"We're the highest taxed nation in the world."* Untrue.[49]

TRUMP'S TAX RETURNS – May 4, 2017 *"Nobody cares about my tax return except for the reporters."* Polls show most Americans do care.[50]

NATO CONTRIBUTIONS – May 8, 2017 *"...we've gotten billions more in NATO...All because of me."* The deal was struck in 2014.[51]

COLBERT'S LATE SHOW RATINGS – May 8,2017 *"...when I did his show... It was ...highest rating he ever had."* Colbert's Late Show debut had nearly two million more viewers.[52]

AIRCRAFT SAVINGS – May 13, 2017 *"I'm cutting the price of airplanes with Lockheed."* Donald, this is getting to be tiresome even if you adjust the language. Most of those cuts were negotiated and planned during the Obama administration.[53]

This was only a sampling of Trump's lies for the first six months of his term. I feel sure he won't disappoint those of us who believe he has only just begun.

Chapter 16 The Election

"In addition to winning the Electoral College in a landslide, I won the popular vote if you deduct the millions of people who voted illegally." It seems at times that Trump sees himself as someone who is the best at everything. While we will pass on that issue; is there anyone more masterful in deceit? In the above quotation of only 25 words, he has managed to tell two lies and cover up at least one other truth and maybe a second. The first lie is that his Electoral College margin was a landslide. That is unequivocally false. Since 1920, only the electoral college margins of 1948, 1976, 2000 and 2004, have been thinner. In other words, out of twenty-five Presidential elections, the election of 2016 was the fifth closest electoral college margin.

Looking more closely at the state by state result reveals something even more interesting. Trump's victory hinged on three states; Pennsylvania, Michigan, and Wisconsin.

The total margin of victory for those three states was 67,744. If you divide that number by two and add three votes, you come up with the number of votes that would have to have been cast for Hillary Clinton instead of Donald Trump. 33, 875 votes out of a total of 137,125,484; or 0.025%. Some landslide victory, huh?

So, the statement that the 2016 electoral college victory was a landslide is not only false; but covers up the fact that it was historically a very thin margin. However, Trump and his supporters will likely accuse me of being unfair After all, it was the third greatest margin since 2000.

Let's move on to the second untruth in his above statement. There is absolutely no evidence of anything approaching wide spread illegal voting; whether by illegal immigrants or otherwise.

The possible second cover up is that Russia may have deliberately swung the election to Trump. There is no way of ever knowing how great an effect that Russia had; but there is plenty of evidence that Russia did indeed attempt to do so.

Chapter 17 Russian Collusion

"It is commonly agreed, after many months of COSTLY looking, that there was NO collusion between Russia and Trump..."@realDonaldTrump Oct 27,2017

No, Donald. It is not commonly agreed unless you are referring to those of your cult who agree with everything you say, which is often self-contradictory. While collusion between Trump himself and the Russian government is yet to be proven; the evidence is mounting. At the very least, we know now that some of his campaign team, including one former member of his administration, were having discussions with Russian officials, regarding "dirt" on Hillary and/or lifting the sanctions against Russia.

Even if Trump did not encourage those contacts or was not personally involved; it is clear that he is feeling the heat as Special Counsel Mueller's investigation moves on to the White House inner circle. As mentioned earlier, Donald's total turnaround on Hillary's "suffering" is one indication; and the other is his obsession with the investigation. The two word phrase *"no collusion"* was used by Donald and White House spokespersons at least 140 times as of January 11, 2018.[1]

Despite the strong denials from Donald, his lawyers, and administration officials of any collusion, it has been positively confirmed by our intelligence services that the Russian government has been involved in an effort to subvert our election process.

Trump and his supporters say that if there was any collusion with the Russians; it was Hillary and the Democrats. So it might be fair to ask why Putin would have had any interest in who our next President would be; or specifically, why he would favor Clinton over Trump. Hillary was Secretary of State in 2014 when the U.S. along with a number of European countries imposed sanctions on Russia. She was outspoken in her support of even more stringent sanctions. It is not totally clear why Putin might have wanted Trump other than the rumored embarrassing information that they had on him in the notorious dossier; but maybe it was that Putin saw in him a political outlier that could be persuaded in a quid pro quo deal. In any event, Trump was quoted in a July 2016 interview by a German reporter that he might be receptive to lifting the sanctions against Russia if he became President.[3] Trump was also quoted as saying that NATO was obsolete,[4] a statement which would not have made Putin unhappy.

Chapter 18 Self – Funding his campaign

To be fair, this lie may just be a misunderstanding of the term *self-funding*. I, and I suspect a lot of other people, thought it meant that he would be paying for his campaign out of his own pocket. Apparently, he has a different conception of what self-funding means.

Back on June 16, 2015, when Donald announced he was running for President; he said, "*I don't need anybody's money. I'm using my own money.*" While he had loaned his campaign $47.9 million[1] through May 2016, Trump's own contributions to his campaign dwindled in comparison to outside donors after he had won enough primaries and caucuses to assure himself the nomination. Between June and August 2016, total receipts to the campaign were $83.1 million.[2] Trump's contributions during that same period were $6.1 million or only about 7% of the total.[3]

Two questions: If he was using his own money, why was he accepting donations? OK. He said he didn't '*need*' it; he didn't say he wouldn't *take* it. But why was he *loaning* his campaign money? Didn't that imply that he expected to be paid back? To be fair, it was reported in August that Trump forgave his loans; but this was only after a lot of pressure to do so.

A final recap as of 12/31/2016 showed that the Trump campaign raised $333 million of which $66 million or 19.85% was self-financed. Individual contributions accounted for 39.69%. PAC contributions only accounted for 0.04%. No Federal funds were used; but there was another category of '*Other*' that is unexplained. If we subtract Trump's loans of $45.7million from the above self-financed category of $66 million; it appears that Trump's out of pocket contribution to his campaign was slightly over $20 million or about 6% of the total collected. I would say that's not bad for self-financing.

But that's not all. A significant amount of campaign spending was to Trump's own businesses. In 2015, the campaign spent more than $2 million for flights on his own planes and helicopter and a quarter of a million dollars to his Fifth Avenue office tower.[4] That is more than one third of the total received from outside donors during that period.[5] I was unable to find an accounting through election day; but for the month of May 2016 alone, the campaign paid at least $1.1 million to his businesses and family members for expenses associated with events and travel costs. The total represents nearly a fifth of the $6 million that his campaign spent in the month.[6]

Furthermore, his website was not taken down after the election. It is still up and running requesting donations to Make America Great Again.

Back in 2000, when he was in his first run for President under the Reform Party label, Trump was quoted in an interview with Fortune Magazine, *"It's very possible that I could be the first presidential candidate to run and make money on it."*[7] As I think that I have made clear, I don't put a lot of stock in most of Trump's statements; but I would bank on this one.

Chapter 19 Ted Cruz

During a campaign debate in May 2016, Donald accused Ted Cruz's father, Rafael, of being involved in President Kennedy's assassination; perhaps, even the shooter on the grassy knoll. As evidence, he cited the National Enquirer story, https://www.politico.com/story/2016/09/donald-trump including a photograph of Lee Harvey Oswald with a group of people handing out pro-Castro leaflets. One unidentified man was allegedly Rafael Cruz. The fact is that Rafael was rabidly anti-Castro even before a savage beating of his sister by Castro forces. But Donald has never let facts get in the way of a juicy story that played well into his assertion that Ted Cruz is not even an American citizen, having been born in Canada; but of an American mother, which according to legal scholars made him a natural born citizen, eligible for the Presidency.

A couple of months earlier The National Enquirer came out with a story alleging the Senator of having affairs with five women. Although Donald didn't specifically state that the allegation was true; he certainly was willing to fan the flames, *"hoping"* <for Heidi's sake> *"that the story was not true." "Ted Cruz's problem with the National Enquirer is his and his alone and while they were right about O.J. Simpson, John Edwards, and many others, I certainly hope they are not right about Lyin' Ted Cruz."*

Does anyone really believe that Donald was sincere in that last sentence?

Chapter 20 Fake News
by David Cholesterol

While riding on the back of *Infowars, The Gateway Pundit, The National Examiner,* and a plethora of conspiracy theory and Russian bot bloggers all the way to the White House, "FAKE NEWS" is a common attack Donald Trump shamelessly implements against every negative news story about him.

"The media is really, the word, one of the greatest of all terms I've come up with, is 'fake,'" Trump told Mike Huckabee in an interview on the Trinity Broadcasting Network. *"I guess other people have used it perhaps over the years but I've never noticed it. And it's a shame. And they really hurt the country. Because they take away the spirit of the country."*

His admirers follow suit, as they scream "FAKE NEWS!" at any and all credible criticism of Trump, while they are the *numero uno* connoisseurs and distributors of actual FAKE NEWS (especially when they get their "fact-based" news from the Liar and Chief himself).

On the topic of "FAKE NEWS", Trump blogger Donna Garner from *"Education Views"* says, *"We can get our fact-based news directly from the President of the United States himself... It is such a joy each morning to go to Pres. Trump's Twitter page and have him talk directly to me, a common, everyday American who wants to know what is really happening in our world in real time."*

For true Conservatives, who have been dealing with these mindless sycophants for the last 2 1/2 years, this is no revelation. However, for posterity, I wish to share a small example of what they are prone to unequivocally believe.

I found this clickbait gem that a Trumper was circulating in a Facebook group called Facebook Conservatives....

The story's grammar-challenged title, "AMERICAN TEENAGE WHOM KILLED MUSLIM REFUGEE FOR RAPING HIS 7 YEARS OLD SISTER SENTENCED 30 YEARS TO LIFE IN A FEDERAL PRISON" comes from a FAKE NEWS site (probably Russian or Macedonian) fallaciously called *"Conservative ONES dot com."*

If you actually go to the website, there are *no* details that the headline insinuates... but rather details about another FAKE story (discredited by Snopes) from 2014 about a teenager who was sentenced to 25 years for "swatting" (the action or practice of making a prank call to emergency services in an attempt to bring about the dispatch of a large number of armed police officers to a particular address). By the way, the **exact** misleading headline and lack of information can also be ironically found at the spyware-plagued website called *American President Donald J. Trump* (*usdeplorableslovestrump* dot com if you want to chance it), in which they ridiculously dub themselves *"A Tested and Trustworthy Team."*

So... even though this was FAKE NEWS on top of FAKE NEWS, many ignorant Trumper members reacted solely to the title, did *no* research of their own, and even shared the FAKE NEWS to their Trumper friends. This sort of reaction is prevalent in Trump groups and groups with the misnomer, "Conservative" in their titles all over Facebook.

While reacting solely to an article's title is a laziness and gullibility not isolated to Trumpists, their relentless "FAKE NEWS" Trump-mimicry exposes their blatantly shameless hypocrisy. Even while perusing most of these faux "conservative" Facebook groups on November 5, 2017; if the top story wasn't about the "evil corrupt Mueller," it was about the Antifa "civil war" that was supposed to happen on November 4, but NEVER happened.

How can a nation survive when many within our electorate abandon reason for madness?

Finally, the indication that Russia contributed greatly to Trump's campaign and continues to feed misinformation throughout social media should not be ignored. As mass distributors of FAKE NEWS, the Russian/Macedonian news sites are permeating both Twitter and Facebook every day, and the Trump cult takes it all in, hook, line and sinker.

It would be nice to think that some members of the Trump cult would read this book and heed; but I regret to say that most likely will not be the case. What we must do is continue to speak out to reach the many who have not yet been infected by this mindless virus.

Chapter 21 *1984*

"War is peace. Freedom is slavery. Ignorance is strength." *"Big Brother is Watching You."* In George Orwell's *1984,* Big Brother had no need to shut down the printing presses. He managed the suppression of the free press by a much more devious and efficient means. He did so by what the book referred to as *Doublethink,* which is defined as the power of holding two contradictory beliefs in one's mind, and accepting both of them simultaneously. By continual repetition of obviously self-contradictory statements, the people eventually lost the power to think and relegated that process to the State.

If there is any doubt as to Donald being the record holder for promises made and broken by a President; it is inconceivable that there has been any president who has even come close to his number of self-contradictions. If there is much of anything in which he has not contradicted himself, other than his professed love of America, I can not recall it. Even on his supposed love of America (and the implication of everything America stands for), his actions betray his words. As a young man, he eluded the draft with several deferments followed by a medical disqualification, based on the flimsy excuse of bone spurs in his heels. After his first State of the Union address, he implied that the Democrats who had not stood and applauded his speech had committed a *"treasonous"* act.

He has attacked the First Amendment by fostering religious discrimination and intolerance of dissenting views in speech and the press. He has attacked people solely based on race and/or country of origin. He has attacked the judiciary because of some contrary judgements and also because of one judge's ethnicity. He has attacked the Department of Justice and our intelligence services as the Russia collusion investigation closes in on the White House. He has asked for personal loyalty pledges from members of the Justice Department and FBI; and he fired the Director of the FBI when the pledge was not forthcoming. Later, he had the Deputy Director of the FBI fired, when the official had the temerity to support his former boss. And, if all of the above weren't enough, he has enabled and encouraged a foreign power to attempt to influence our elections. Now, he wants to have a military parade to flaunt his patriotism and probably, if he thought he could get away with it, lead the parade sitting atop a tank in the uniform he spurned during a war when it really counted.

Whether or not he initiated the collusion with Russia on the 2016 election, it is clear that Trump became aware of it; did nothing to bring it to an end; and even encouraged that government to continue into the future through his denials and close friendship with President Vladimir Putin. The apparent explanation for Putin's interest in getting Trump elected, was a *quid pro quo* on the sanctions on Russia imposed by the U.S. and allies for its aggression in Ukraine. Trump has been attempting to fulfill his end of the bargain by lifting the sanctions, which thankfully, Congress has opposed. Further sanctions, as a result of Russia tampering in the 2016 election, have been blocked by Trump and his surrogates in Congress.

Trump on many issues reminds me of Tevya in *Fiddler On the Roof,* in his self-dialogue, *"On the other hand..."* Here is the classic Trump doublethink: *"The day I realized it can be smart to be shallow was, for me, a deep experience."* [1] That certainly requires some deep thought. In other words, being shallow can be deep; and I guess the converse may be true (or false). And how about this one?

"Sometimes—not often, but sometimes—less is more." [2] (But on second thought,) *"I always say, 'More is more.'"*[3] And while we are on the subject of deep thought: *"I'm a thinker, and I have been a thinker. ... I'm a very deep thinker."* [4] Furthermore, *"Actually, throughout my life, my two greatest assets have been mental stability and like, really smart. I think that would qualify as not smart, but genius...and a very stable genius at that."* [5] (But, of course,) *"<you> never want people to think you're a loser or a schlepper, but it's not a good idea if they think you're the smartest guy in the room, either."* [6]

"I avoid people with especially high opinions of their own abilities or worth." [7]

"Hey, look, I went to the hardest school to get into, the best school in the world, I guess you could say, the Wharton School of Finance. It's like super genius stuff. I came out. I built a tremendous company. I had tremendous success." [8] (But)*"Do not look for approval from others. That is a sure sign of weakness."* [9]

"Look at my hands. ... My hands are normal hands. During a debate, he <Rubio> was losing, and he said, 'Oh, he has small hands and therefore, you know what that means.'..OK? So, he started it. So, what I said a couple of days later ... and what happened is, I was on line shaking hands with supporters, and one of the supporters got up and he said, 'Mr. Trump, you have strong hands. You have good-sized hands.' And then another one would say, 'You have great hands, Mr. Trump, I had no idea.' I said, 'What do you mean?' He said, 'I thought you were,

like, deformed, and I thought you had small hands.' I had 50 people. ... I mean, people were writing, 'How are Mr. Trump's hands?' My hands are fine. You know, my hands are normal. Slightly large, actually. In fact, I buy a slightly smaller than large glove, OK?" [10]

Here's another good one: *"It's always good to do things nice and complicated so that nobody can figure it out."* [11]

Trump may be credited with creating the phrase, *FAKE NEWS;* but true only in exact wording. Hitler used the term, *Luegenpresse,* which translates to "Lying press". Our First Amendment is not in first place by accident. Freedom of the press and freedom of speech are the first bulwarks against a would be dictator. If people stop believing the news; it is as effective as shutting the news down.

At a 2016 campaign stop in Miami with an audience of Haitians, Donald proclaimed if elected that he would be their *"greatest champion and I will be your champion."* [12] Pair that with his remarks previously cited at the bi-partisan White House meeting on January 11, 2018. *"Why are we having all these people from shit-hole countries <like Haiti> come here." "Why do we need more Haitians?"*

His cult will likely reply, *"Can't a fellow change his mind?"* During a press conference in Palm Beach Florida, Donald may have explained it when he said, *"There are probably two Donald Trumps, the public version and people see that and I don't know what they see exactly; but it seems to have worked over my lifetime. But it's probably different, I think, than the personal Donald Trump."* [13]

But moments later, in response to a reporter's question about the two Donald Trumps, the other Donald must have appeared and replied, *"I don't think there are two Donald Trumps. I think there is one Donald Trump."* [14]

"I am me." [15]

"What I say is what I say." [16]

Donald, with all due respect, some people see you as an enigma. Would you care to define yourself?

"Define yourself in a big way. We all have self-definitions; give yourself a big definition." [17]

"I tend to do what I do." [18] *"I do it to do it."* [19] *"I'm never self-satisfied."* [20] (However,) *"In truth I am dazzled as much by my own creations as are the tourists and glamour hounds that flock to Trump Tower."* [21] *"If I were satisfied, I would not be Donald Trump."* [22] *"I have an organization but it's largely myself."* [23] *"You are what you think you are."* [24] *"I'm Swedish."* [25] *"I'm proud to have that German blood. Great stuff."* [26]

OK. Now that that has been resolved, where does Donald (or Donalds, as the case may be) stand on the issues?

Trump's hottest button issue with his base has been illegal immigration and yet, just six years ago, he was criticizing Mitt Romney for taking such a hard line approach. [26] In an interview with Bill O'Reilly in 2011, Trump responded to a question on what he would do with the fifteen million illegal immigrants by saying that each case should be decided individually on some type of merit based program. [27]

Regarding ISIS and Syria. ***"Allow Russia to deal with the Islamic State in Syria** and/or work with Russian President Vladimir Putin to wipe out shared enemies."* [28]

(And/or???) *"I have always felt that Russia and the United States should be able to work well with each other."* [29] *"President Trump? He would believe very strongly in extreme military strength. He wouldn't trust anyone. He wouldn't trust the Russians."* [30]

"I see NATO as a good thing." [31] (But, maybe not.)*"I think NATO is obsolete."* [32] **(I'm sure Putin would agree.)** *"In favor of invading Iraq? Yeah, I guess so."* [33]

"It looks like a tremendous success from a military standpoint." [34]

(However,) *"The war's a mess."* [35]

"Qadhafi in Libya is killing thousands of people, nobody knows how bad it is, and we're sitting around, we have soldiers, all over the Middle East, and we're not bringing 'em in to stop this horrible carnage. ... We should go in, we should stop this guy, which would be very easy and very quick." [36]

"I never discussed that subject. I was in favor of Libya? We would be so much better off if Qadhafi were in charge right now." [37]

On March 18, 2018, Trump tweeted, *"We call for the full restoration of democracy and political freedom in Venezuela, and we want it to happen very very soon."* Two days later, Trump called Russian President Valdimir Putin to congratulate him on his re-election. During a White House press briefing following that phone call, Sarah Huckabee Sanders, the Press Secretary was asked, *"Is the White House stance* (tacitly, referring to Trump's congratulatory phone call) *that the election in Russia was free and fair?"* Sanders replied, *"It is not up to us* to determine how someone else handles their elections." Too bad that there was not a follow-up question. (*Does that just apply to countries other than Venezuela?*) OK, let's move on to the issue of abortion.

"Look, I'm very pro-choice. I hate the concept of abortion. I hate it. I hate everything it stands for. I cringe when I listen to people debating the subject, but you still—I just believe in choice. ... I am strongly for choice, and yet I hate the concept of abortion. ... I am pro-choice in every respect ... but I just hate it." 38

"My position has not changed- like Ronald Reagan, I am pro-life with exceptions." 39

"I am very, very proud to say that I'm pro-life." 40

(With or without exceptions?) During a townhall meeting in Green Bay, Wisconsin, sponsored by MSNBC, Chris Matthews in a followup to a woman's question asked Trump what sort of punishment a woman should receive for having an abortion. With a lot of dodging, finally Matthews got Trump to agree that there should be some unspecified yet to be determined punishment for the woman. Hours later, Donald clarified his position on Twitter.

"If Congress were to pass legislation making abortion illegal and the federal courts upheld this legislation, or any state were permitted to ban abortion under state and federal law, the doctor or any other person performing this illegal act upon a woman would be held legally responsible, not the woman ..." 41

If Matthews could get Trump on his show for a followup interview, which is unlikely; he should ask the President what sort of punishment should be given if a woman takes a pill obtained from a foreign source to induce abortion. *"But Planned Parenthood should absolutely be defunded. I mean, if you look at what's going on with that, it's terrible."*[42] (Nevertheless,) *"Millions and millions of women—cervical cancer, breast cancer—are helped by Planned Parenthood. So you can say whatever you want, but they have millions of women going through Planned Parenthood that are helped greatly."* [43]

How about the issue of gay marriage?

"I'm against gay marriage." [44] *"I think the institution of marriage should be between a man and a woman."* [45] (But, on the other hand,) *"If two people dig each other, they dig each other."* [46] *"It's like in golf. A lot of people—I don't want this to sound trivial—but a lot of people are switching to these really long putters, very unattractive. It's weird. You see these great players with these really long putters, because they can't sink three-footers anymore. And I hate it. I am a traditionalist. I have so many fabulous friends who happen to be gay, but I am a traditionalist."* [47]

Thanks, Donald, for clearing that up. Now, let's move on to traditional marriage. Would you consider yourself a good husband?

"Being on the other side of a relationship with someone like me must be difficult."[48] *"But there is nothing better than having a great marriage, in my opinion. There is nothing more beautiful, and there is nothing more important."* [49] *"You marry for love, but your signature on the marriage certificate is all about rights, duties, and property. It's a legally binding contract that knows nothing of love."* [50] *"I think I've been a very good husband."*[51] (But,) *"What the hell do I know, I've been*

divorced twice?" [52] "Believe it or not, I'm a romantic guy."[53]

"Geraldo Rivera is a friend of mine, but he did something which I thought was absolutely terrible and he admits it was a mistake. He wrote a book naming many of the famous women that he slept with. I would never do that—I have too much respect for women in general, but if I did, the world would take serious notice. Beautiful, famous, successful, married—I've had them all, secretly, the world's biggest names, but unlike Geraldo I don't talk about it." [54] "I don't have to brag. I don't have to. Believe it or not." [55]

And how about children?

"I've never been the kind of guy who takes his son out to Central Park to play catch, but I think I'm a good father." [56] " I like kids. I mean, I won't do anything to take care of 'em. I'll supply funds, and she'll take care of the kids." [57]

With all the shootings, where do you stand on gun control?

"I generally oppose gun control, but I support the ban on assault weapons and I support a slightly longer waiting period to purchase a gun." [58] (However,)"I am the strongest person running in favor of the Second Amendment."[59] "My sons love to hunt. They are members of the NRA, very proudly. I am a big believer in the Second Amendment."[60] (On the other hand,) "I'm not a hunter and don't approve of killing animals. I strongly disagree with my sons who are hunters." [61]

Where do you stand on protection of private property, specifically, eminent domain?

"Eminent domain is wonderful." [62] (but,)"I don't like eminent domain." [63]

So, Donald. In view of your positions on those and other

issues; would you call yourself a conservative, liberal, or something in between?

"If I ever ran for office, I'd do better as a Democrat than as a Republican—and that's not because I'd be more liberal, because I'm conservative." [64] *"I'm a registered Republican. I'm a pretty conservative guy. (,although) I'm somewhat liberal on social issues, especially health care."* [65] *"I've actually been an activist Democrat and Republican."* [66] *"You'd be shocked if I said that in many cases I probably identify more as a Democrat."* [67] *"Look, I'm a Republican. I'm a very conservative guy in many respects—I guess in most respects."* [68] *"Folks, I'm a conservative, but at this point, who cares? We got to straighten out the country."* [69]

You sure sound like a politician.

"Politicians are all talk and no action." [70] *"I'm no different than a politician running for office."* [71] (However,)*"I'm not a politician."* [72]

Donald, since you obviously have an extraordinary mind; do you rely on advisors or prefer to go with your gut?

"You're generally better off sticking with what you know." [73] (But, then again,)*"I couldn't be a one-man show…"* [74] *"Don't think you're so smart that you can go it alone."* [75] *"I surround myself with good people, and then I give myself the luxury of trusting them."* [76] (But,)*"People are too trusting. I'm a very untrusting guy."* [77] *"Think of yourself as a one-man army."* [78] *"You must plan and execute your plan alone."* [79] (On the other hand,)*"It's essential that you keep your mind open and alert."* [80] *"Surround yourself with people you can trust."* [81] *"You know, I know the smart people. I really know the smart people. I deal with the smart people."* [82] (But,)*"If you have smart people*

working for you, they'll try to screw you if they think they can do better without you."[83] *"My motto is 'Hire the best people, and don't trust them.'"*[84] *"I do listen to people. I hire experts. I hire top, top people. And I do listen."* [85] (Nevertheless,) *"I'm speaking with myself, No. 1, because I have a very good brain and I've said a lot of things. ... My primary consultant is myself."*[86]

So where do you get your information?

"All I know is what's on the Internet." [87]*"Fortunately, I don't pride myself on being a know-it-all."*[88] (But,) *"I've cultivated the learning habit over the years, and it's one of the most pleasurable aspects of my life."* [89] (Also,)*"Small talk can be one of the best ways to educate yourself."* [90] (However,) *"I can't stand small talk."* [91]

"It would take an hour and a half to learn everything there is to learn about missiles. ... I think I know most of it anyway." [92] *"I <also> know more about ISIS than the generals do."*

"Well, I read a lot ... and over my life, I've read so much." [93] (But, maybe not after all.) *"I don't read much. Mostly I read contracts, but usually my lawyers do most of the work. There are too many pages."* [94] *"I actually love watching television."* [95] (But?)*"I don't have a lot of time for listening to television."* [96]

Donald, with all due respect, it seems that you have an aversion to most of the media. Would you care to comment?

"I continue to alienate members of the press on occasion, but on the whole, I like them." [97] *"They are the most dishonest people in the world. The media. They are the worst. They are very dishonest people. They are terrible."* [98] *"OK, no, I don't hate anybody. I love the media. They're wonderful."* [99] *"I guess*

we wouldn't be here, maybe, if it wasn't for the media, so maybe we shouldn't be complaining." [100]

Well, after you feel that you have the information you need on a particular subject; how do you arrive at a decision?

"The simplest approach is often the most effective." [101] *"I prefer to come to work each day and just see what develops."* [102] (On the other hand,)*"You can't just sit around waiting for deals, opportunities, or a lucky break."* [103] *"I look at things for the art sake and the beauty sake and for the deal sake."* [104] *"I see no value whatsoever in believing ignorance to be an attribute."* [105] (On the other hand,) *"I love the poorly educated."* [106]

Who are your favorite people, Donald?

"I like (and dislike) all sorts of people—winners, losers, and those in the middle!" [107] *"You'll find that when you become very successful, the people that you will like best are the people that are less successful than you, because when you go to a table you can tell them all of these wonderful stories, and they'll sit back and listen. Does that make sense to you? Always be around unsuccessful people because everybody will respect you."* [108] *"The world is a vicious and brutal place. We think we're civilized. In truth, it's a cruel world and people are ruthless. They act nice to your face, but underneath they're out to kill you. ... Even your friends are out to get you: they want your job, they want your house, they want your money, they want your wife, and they even want your dog. Those are your friends; your enemies are even worse!"* [109]

How about some specific people?

"Jimmy Carter. After he lost the election to Ronald Reagan,

Carter came to see me in my office. He told me he was seeking contributions to the Jimmy Carter Library. I asked how much he had in mind. And he said, 'Donald, I would be very appreciative if you contributed five million dollars.' I was dumbfounded. I didn't even answer him.

"But that experience also taught me something. Until then, I'd never understood how Jimmy Carter became president. The answer is that as poorly qualified as he was for the job, Jimmy Carter had the nerve, the guts, the balls, to ask for something extraordinary. That ability above all helped him get elected president." [110] *"... . He <Jimmy Carter> is a very nice man, but he wasn't my kind of president. I was more into the Ronald Reagans of the world. Nevertheless, after President Carter's term as President was up, he asked to meet me and of course I agreed. I didn't know what he wanted in that I had never supported him and was actually very vocal on how poorly he handled our captives in Iran. ... Nevertheless, we had a wonderful conversation prior to getting to his point, which was, would I consider making a $50 million contribution to the Jimmy Carter Library? Here was a man that I had not supported, had not voted for, and yet he was in my office asking for a $50 million contribution! I said to myself, and I told the story many times, that Jimmy Carter, despite his image to the contrary, had an ability to think big. That's why he ran for President and others did not."* [111]

"Ronald Reagan ... is so smooth and so effective a performer that he completely won over the American people. Only now, nearly seven years later, are people beginning to question whether there's anything beneath that smile." [112] *"... Reagan, to me, was a great president. And whether you are liberal or you're conservative, people really view him as a great*

president. He'll go down as a great president and not so much for the things he did, it's just, there was a demeanor to him and a spirit that the country had under Ronald Reagan that was really phenomenal. And, you know, there was just a style and a class ... I mean, that's a really big part of being president. Ronald Reagan had it." [113]

"George W. Bush? I like him."[114] *"Don't talk to me about Bush, I was never a defender or a fan!"* [115]

"I like John McCain." [116] *"I'm not a fan of John McCain."* [117]

"Ron Paul has some serious ideas which deserve serious consideration. Wrong for media to ignore him." "He should be ignored. @RonPaul's foreign policy is a dream come true for our enemies. He has zero chance to beat @BarackObama. " [118]

Mitt Romney "is the steady conservative who can restore America's future." [119] *"He's <Romney> a jealous fool and not a bright person. He's good looking. Other than that, he's got nothing."* [120]

George Pataki is "the most underrated guy in American politics." [121] *"..Pataki was a terrible governor of NY, one of the worst- would have been swamped if he ran again. . couldn't be elected dog catcher if he ran again- so he didn't."* [122]

"Jeb Bush is a good man. I've held fundraisers for him. He's exactly the kind of political leader this country needs now and will very much need in the future. He, too, knows how to hang in there. His first shot at Florida's governorship didn't work out, but he didn't give up. He was campaigning the day after his loss. He won the next race in a landslide. He's bright, tough, and principled."[123] *"He's like a lost soul, Jeb Bush ... this poor, pathetic, low-energy guy."* [124]

"Here's a man <Barack Obama> that not only got elected, I think he's doing a really good job...Oh, yes, he's a champion. I mean, he won against all odds. If you would have looked— when he first announced, people were giving him initially no chance. And he's just done something that's amazing. He's totally a champion." [125] *"Barack Obama has been the worst president ever."* [126] *"Barack Obama is not who you think he is."* [127]

"Hillary Clinton is definitely smart and resilient." [128] *"Incompetent Hillary doesn't know what she's talking about. She doesn't have a clue. She's made such bad decisions."* [129] *"I know Hillary and I think she'd make a great president ..."* [130] *"Hillary will be a disaster as a president."* [131] *"I think that a lot of people will be looking at Hillary's record as secretary of state, and she will be defending that, and I'm sure she'll do a good job of defending it."* [132] *"She was the worst secretary of state in the history of our nation. There's never been a secretary of state so bad as Hillary."* [133]

"Angela Merkel is doing a fantastic job ... Youth unemployment is at a record low & she has a budget surplus." [134] *She's "ruining Germany."* [135]

John Kerry is "a very solid and stand-up guy." [136] *"Obviously Kerry did not read The Art of the Deal."* [137]

Donald, you have been so successful. Is it due to the power of positive thinking or something else?

"I believe in positive thinking, but I also believe in the power of negative thinking." [138] *"I never think of the negative."* [139] *"I always go into the deal anticipating the worst."* [140] *"I believe in the power of positive thinking, but I never like to talk about it."* [141] *"I don't think positively, I don't think negatively."* [142] *"I'm a*

very happy man."[143] (But, on the other hand) *"I'm not the world's happiest person."* [144] *"The worst hell you will ever face is the hell you create with your own mind."* [145] *"Stop the indecisive internal dialogue before it starts. That is your biggest enemy."*[146] *"I'm walking, talking proof of the American Dream. For me, the American Dream is not just a dream; it's a reality."*[147] (But maybe not?) *"The American Dream is dead."*[148] *"Maybe we Americans pump ourselves up too much."* [149] *"We are the greatest country the world has ever known."* [150] *"I don't worry about anything."* [151] *"But I often think of nuclear war. I've always thought about the issue of nuclear war; it's a very important element in my thought process. It's the ultimate, the ultimate catastrophe, the biggest problem this world has, and nobody's focusing on the nuts and bolts of it. It's a little like sickness. People don't believe they're going to get sick until they do. Nobody wants to talk about it. I believe the greatest of all stupidities is people's believing it will never happen, because everybody knows how destructive it will be, so nobody uses weapons. What bullshit. On a much lower level, I would never hire anybody who thinks that way, because he has absolutely no common sense. He's living in a world of make-believe. It's like thinking the Titanic can't sink. Too many countries have nuclear weapons; nobody knows where they're all pointed, what button it takes to launch them. The bomb Harry Truman dropped on Hiroshima was a toy next to today's. We have thousands of weapons pointed at us and nobody even knows if they're going to go in the right direction. They've never really been tested. These jerks in charge don't know how to paint a wall, and we're relying on them to shoot nuclear missiles to Moscow. What happens if they don't go there? What happens if our computer systems aren't working? Nobody knows if this equipment works, and I've seen numerous reports lately stating that the probability is they don't work. It's a total mess."* [152] *"I'm really concerned with the whole earthquake situation in L.A. I am a tremendous believer that someday Las Vegas may be the West Coast. ... People in general are having lingering doubts about the value of real estate in L.A. It's happening too much and too often, the tremors. It's a very scary thing."* [153] (However,) *"L.A. is going to be very hot, and it is very hot. The fact that Trump goes there makes it even hotter."* [154]

OK, Donald. You are a positive thinker; but with all your success, you've also had some losers. How does that make you feel?

"I don't like to lose." [155] *"Anyone who thinks he's going to win them all is going to wind up a big loser."* [156] (However,) *"I win, I win, I always win. In the end I always win, whether it's in golf, whether it's in tennis, whether it's in life, I just always win. And I tell people I always win, because I do."* [157] *"I do whine, because I want to win, and I'm not , about not winning, and I am a whiner, and I keep whining and whining until I win."* [158] *"Toughness is knowing how to be a gracious winner— and rebounding quickly when you lose."* [159] *"I want to make America great again, and you can't do that if you come in a close second."* [160] *"We finished second, and I want to tell you something: I'm just honored. I'm really honored."* [161] *"You hear lots of people say that a great deal is when both sides win. That is a bunch of crap."* [162] (However,) *"Remember that in the best negotiations, everyone wins."* [163] (But,) *"I'm not big on compromise. I understand compromise. Sometimes compromise is the right answer, but oftentimes compromise is the equivalent of defeat, and I don't like being defeated."* [164]

(However,)*"Compromise is not a dirty word."* [165]

Everybody screws up occasionally. How do you deal with it?

"I do something wrong—I do things wrong—and when I do, I don't mind."[166] (But,) *"It's amazing how often I am right."* [167] *"You can't con people, at least not for long. You can create excitement, you can do wonderful promotion and get all kinds of press, and you can throw in a little hyperbole. But if you don't deliver the goods, people will eventually catch on."* [167]

OK, Donald. So what would you advise someone aspiring to be an entrepreneur?

"When you shake somebody's hand, go with it. It is very important. Shaking hands with someone means you are making a deal." [168] *"Some business executives believe in a firm handshake. (However,)I believe in no handshake. It is a terrible practice. So often, I see someone who is obviously sick, with a bad cold or the flu, who approaches me and says, 'Mr. Trump, I would like to shake your hand.' It's a medical fact that this is how germs are spread."* [169]

(Also,) *"Stay as close to home as possible. Travel is time-consuming and, in my opinion, boring—especially compared with the fun I have doing deals in my office. I can never understand people who say that if they had a lot of money they would spend their time traveling. It's just not my thing."* [170] *"There's no excuse for staying home; the world's too fantastic to miss out on it. I wish I could travel more."* [171]

"Dress the part and act the part. Do not cause any doubt in anybody's mind that you don't know your stuff. When I moved to Manhattan to do my first deal, I did not have money or employees. When I went into an office, I acted as if I had an

organization, The Trump Organization, behind me. I was on my own and no longer working for my father. Few people knew that The Trump Organization had no employees except myself and operated out of my studio apartment in Manhattan." [172] (On the other hand,) *"Sometimes people will come into my office and they will be great. They will look great, they'll sound great, they dress beautifully; everything is great. Then after you hire them they turn out to be morons. Sometimes a real slob will come in looking for a job. He does not dress well. He does not look good. He does not seem to be very smart. It turns out when you hire him or her, you find out you have hired a genius."* [173]

"I learned from my father that work can make you happy." [174] *"I think of it almost as a controlled neurosis, which is a quality I've noticed in many highly successful entrepreneurs. They're obsessive, they're driven, they're single-minded and sometimes they're almost maniacal, but it's all channeled into their work. ... I don't say this trait leads to a happier life, or a better life, but it's great when it comes to getting what you want."* [175]

"Let people know what you've done. What good is it if no one knows about it? You've gotta be a promoter." [176] *"Everyone says, 'Oh, Trump is a great promoter.' I don't think I'm even a good promoter."* [177] *"Subtlety and modesty are appropriate for nuns and therapists."* [178] *"So don't be afraid to toot your own horn when you've done something worth tooting about."* [179] *"If I get my name in the paper, if people pay attention, that's what matters. To me, that means it's a success."* [180] (However,) *"Publicity gradually dehumanizes you."* [181] (On the other hand) *"Don't worry about actively promoting yourself."* [182]

"It's fame itself that bends people out of shape. In fact, the more celebrities I meet, the more I realize that fame is a kind of drug, one that is way too powerful for most people to handle." [183]

"I have learned that entertainment is a very simple business. You can be a horrible human being, you can be a truly terrible person, but if you get ratings, you are a king." [184] *"Everybody kisses your ass when you're hot. If you're not hot, they don't even call. So it's always good to stay hot."* [185]

"I hate people that think they're hot stuff, and they're nothing." [186] *"I like it when people talk about me. As long as it is positive."* [187] *"I don't mind being criticized. I'll never, ever complain."* [188] (Well, not really.) *"I really value my reputation and I don't hesitate to sue."* [189]

Along that line, I suspect that you do not take kindly to someone who crosses you?

"When someone crosses you, my advice is 'Get even!' That is not typical advice, but it is real-life advice. If you do not get even, you are just a schmuck! When people wrong you, go after those people, because it is a good feeling and because other people will see you doing it. I love getting even. I get screwed all the time. I go after people, and you know what? People do not play around with me as much as they do with others. They know that if they do, they are in for a big fight. Always get even. Go after people that go after you. Don't let people push you around. Always fight back and always get even. It's a jungle out there, filled with bullies of all kinds who will try to push you around. (What an irony!!) *If you're afraid to fight back people will think of you as a loser, a 'schmuck!' They will know they can get away with insulting you, disrespecting you, and taking*

advantage of you. Don't let it happen! Always fight back and get even." (But) *"If you can avoid an altercation, do so."* (On the other hand) *"If someone attacks you, do not hesitate. Go for the jugular."*[190]

"I don't want to be provocative, and in many cases I try not to be provocative."[191] (But, come to think of it,) *"I do love provoking people. There is truth to that."*[192] *"Sometimes, part of making a deal is denigrating your competition."*[193] (But) *"If striving for wholeness means diminishing your competition, then your competition wasn't much to begin with."* [194]

"Be tough, be smart, be personable, but don't take things personally."[195] *"It makes me feel so good to hit 'sleazebags' back."* [196] *"If you see somebody getting ready to throw a tomato, knock the crap out of 'em, would you? Seriously. OK? Just knock the hell—I promise you, I will pay the legal fees, I promise, I promise."* [197]*"I do not condone violence in any shape."* [198] *"You've gotta be nice."*[199] (On the other hand,) *"I do believe in hate when it's appropriate."* [200] *"I think I am a nice person."*[201] (Although,) *"I'm no angel."* [202] (But,) *"People who know me like me."*[203]

Donald, would you like to sum up?

"If you equivocate, it's an indication that you're unsure of yourself and what you're doing. It's also what politicians do all the time, and I find it inappropriate, insulting and condescending. I try not to do it."[204]

There you have it in Donald's own words. I totally agree with his first sentence and most of the second sentence; and I am sure the cult members agree as well, since there is nothing they disagree with that comes out of his mouth. There may be some who seem to disagree with everything he says or does; but that is disingenuous. I actually agree with about 50% of what he says; since he's on both sides of most issues.

DISCLOSURE: All Trump quotes are actual quotes; however, for purposes of humor, the quotations are not necessarily in chronological order. Also, as should be apparent, the author's comments in parentheses are not to indicate that there was an actual conversation between the author and Trump.

P.S. See appendix for a Trumpspeak glossary.

Conclusion

If you have been paying attention, there is an ominous echo from the past. The people were angry and frustrated; feeling that they were being exploited by the ruling class. And then came a charismatic outsider who promised to make the country great again by cleaning up the corruption and getting rid of a certain group of people that were causing the problems. Today, it is two groups-the Muslims and the undocumented immigrants, mainly Mexican; but the techniques of scapegoating and attacking the press are similar enough to that earlier period to give cause for great concern.

When I posted the above in Face Book under the title of *Echoes of Mein Kampf* over a year ago; the outcry from several fellow Jews was shrill. How dare I compare President Trump to Adolf Hitler, who was responsible for the murder of six million Jews and countless others who were either deemed unfit to live; or who dared to challenge his power?

Most of this book has been a parody on Trump and his followers; and I hope that it has elicited some laughs. Nevertheless, if we ignore the threat that this man poses to our Republic; we do so at great risk. Brian Klass, in his excellent book, *The Despot's Apprentice,* points out that Trump at this stage is not a despot; but he is learning fast.

Despots all use the same techniques. They scapegoat a minority. They build up their favored group by giving them perks and continually telling them how great they are. They attack the press and free speech. They engage in nepotism. They denigrate legitimate law enforcement and they jail their opponents. At this point, Trump is only threatening Hillary; but if I were she, I think I would be worried.

It is scary, indeed. But there is hope. Trump's approval ratings are in the low 30's, which says that the minds of the great majority of the population have not yet been infected by the mass hysteria. However, time is of the essence. It is incumbent on those of us who see the danger to speak out and alert those who view Trump as only an eccentric figure that will pass from the scene when his term or terms end. I hear too many people saying that they didn't vote for him, don't really like him; but that he is doing some good things. It is important to point out that this is the method of would be dictators to latch on to popular sentiment; but at the same time garner more and more control by first usurping the free press.

Appendix

Tax calculations
Family A

calendar year 2017   2018

income   85,000   85,000

personal exemptions 16,600   0

itemized deductions 24,000   standard deduction 24,000

taxable income   44,400   61,000

tax (before credit)

$1865+(25750 \times .15)=$ **5727.5** $1905 + (41950 \times .12)=$ **6939**

child tax credit   2,000   4,000

tax due   **$3727.5**   **$2939**

Savings 3727.5-2939= 768.5 or 21.2%

Family B

calendar year 2017   2018

income   85,000   85,000

personal exemptions 8,300   0

itemized deductions 24,000   standard deduction 24,000

taxable income   52,700   61,000

tax

$1865+ (34050 \times .15)=$ **6972.5** $1905 + (41,950 \times .12)=$ **6939**

Savings 6972.5-6939= $33.5 or 0.48%

Family C

calendar year 2017   2018

income   85,000   85,000

personal exemptions 8,300   0

itemized deductions 30,000   30,000

taxable income   46,700   55,000

tax

1865+ (28050x.15)=**6072.5**   1905 + (35,950x.12)= **6219**

Penalty 6072.5-6219 = − 146.5 or − 2.41%

Glossary

Since it is difficult at times to understand what Trump is saying; I thought it might be helpful to have a glossary of terms in Trumpspeak.

A. **Apology**: A loser admitting he's a loser.

B. **Boasting or bragging**: It's not bragging when you can do it.

C. **Charity**: Contributions of money to worthwhile causes that support me or assist me in achieving certain goals. This can be done with my own money, or more preferably, with Foundation money, which is mostly OPM. Example: The contribution to Florida Attorney General, Pam Bondi's re-election campaign to assist in resolving certain legal problems, involving Trump University.

D. **David Duke**: Wasn't his sister an actress that played that deaf and dumb girl from my favorite state? Also, **Deal:** An agreement where the other guy thinks he is screwing me, and he is the one getting screwed.

E. **Economists**: People that think they know a lot about money.

F. **Fake news**: Generally shown in print as FAKE NEWS: Most mainstream media that attacks me. Antonym: **Real news**. Examples: Anything on my Twitter and most of what's on Fox News.

G. **Genius:** Very, very smart, like me. Also, **Great:** Sometimes shown as greatest- Anything about me.

H. **Humble:** Me, pretending I'm not the greatest. Also ,**Hypocrite**: Person that says he agrees with me and then disagrees with me when I change my mind.

I. **Idiot:** Someone dumber than a Moron. Also, **Inflation:** A way to make more money. And, particularly good when using leverage; since even if you pay the loan back, it's with cheaper money.

J. **Journalists:** Enemies of the state, except Fox News. Also, **Justice:** Pardons for those loyal to me and prison for some of my political opponents.

K. **Kleptocracy:** A seemingly contagious malady that scientists at the CDC have been banned from mentioning.

L. **Leverage:** Using OPM

M. **Modesty**: See Humble. Also, **Moron:** Someone who doesn't understand me. See idiot.

N. **Nepotism:** Family values.

O. **OPM**: Other people's money. The best way to invest or donate.

P. **Philanthropy**: See charity. Also **Promise:** Something like a prediction that may or may not occur in the future.

Q. **Quack:** Any doctor that tells you that I am mentally unfit to be President. Even someone with half his brain tied behind his back knows that I am one of the smartest, most stable people he has ever met. Modesty prevents me from saying more.

R. **Reform:** Changing a system to benefit guess who. Example: Tax reform- Allowing wealthy individuals to keep more of their money to benefit the economy.

S. **Self-funding**: Just as the word implies. Funding one-self with OPM.

T. **Transparency**: The ability to see what I want you to see. Synonym: Opacity

U. **Universe:** As in Ms. Universe, a term I coined for my beauty pageant, featuring the most beautiful young women in the world that let me in their dressing room to inspect the merchandise, strike that. To check everything out. Also, **Useless:** The First Amendment

V. **Vanity:** There is no point in hiding it when you have it.

W. **White Nationalists**: People from Norway and certain other countries that we would like to have more immigration from. Second meaning: People that agree with me on immigration.

X. **Xenophobia:** Xenophobia? Bullshit, I have friends that are Buddhist and they are big into xen.

Y. **Yokel:** I personally don't like the term; but some of my biggest support comes from yokel territory.

Z. **Zen:** Alternate spelling of xen.

DISCLOSURE: To preclude the potential of libel, the above glossary was written "tongue-in-cheek".

Notes

Introduction

1. The Mass Psychology of Fascism by Wilhelm Reich – https://pdfs.semanticscholar.org/61be/0a1790db0e247c30c367fc 29c2d4407237a0.pdf

Chapter 2 Leadership

1. October 16, 2017 Washington Post

Chapter 3 The *Businessman*

1. *NBC's Today* Show – Town Hall Meeting October 26/2015

2. http://www.newsweek.com/authors/kurt-eichenwald 2/14/17

3. https://www.ft.com/content/8c6d9dca-882c-11e7-

4. Ibid.

5. Politico 9/27/2016 Annie Karni

6. *USA Today*/Elections 6/9/2016

7. *Esquire* 1/13/2016

8. *Boston Globe.com* 5/27/2016

9. *www.nytimes.com* 11/19/2016

10. *www.redstate.com* 2/28/2016

11. www.crainsnewyork.com/undoing – *of-Trump-Mortgage*

12. *thinkprogress.org March 4, 2016*

13. *https://www.huffingtonpost.com/*Mar 17, 2017

14. *Washington Post politics 12/27/2017*

15. *USA Today news Sept 6, 2017*

16. CNBC 1/25/2017

17. Washington post .politics 8/10/2017

18. Washington Post.trump hotel – business. 8/7/2017

19. NPR.sections.parallels 2/25/2017

20. https://www.npr.org/2017/01/28/511996783/how-does-trumps-immigration-freeze-square-with-his-business-interests

21. Ibid.

Chapter 4 Inferiority Complex

1. @realDonald Trump Jan 6, 2018

2. *Ibid.*

3. *St. Charles, Missouri speech 11/29/2017*

4. *https://www.usatoday.com/.../09/10/trump-fiorina-look-face/71992454*

5. *https://www.washingtonpost.com/news/post-politics/wp/2016/10/14/...*

6. *https://www.cnn.com/2018/02/26/politics/trump-florida-school...*

Chapter 5 Charity

1. http://www.msn.com/en-us/news/politics/trump-boasts about-his-philanthropy-but his giving-falls-short of his words/ar-AAjAzpL

2. xhttps://www.politico.com/story/2016/06/donald-trump-charities-fraud-laws-224510

3. *https://www.washingtonpost.com/opinions/even-trumps-charity-is-a...*

4. *Ibid.*

5. *https://qz.com/779900/**melania-trump-bid-20000**-on-a-massive*

6. *https://news.**art**net.com/**art**-world/donald-**trump**-bought-portrait...*

7. *https://www.washingtonpost.com/opinions/even-trumps-charity-is-a...*

8. *http://www.slate.com/blogs/the_slatest/2016/09/12/the_trump_foundation_is_just_a_front_for_trump_to_pretend_to_give_to_charity.html*

9. *https://**www.washingtonpost.com**/.../**trump**-charity-donations*

10. **www.independent.co.uk** › *News* › *World* › *Americas* › *US politics*

11. *Buzz Feed News Trump Bought $120,000 Luxury Trip With Trump Foundation Money At 2008 Charity Auction*

12. www.politifact.com/.../donald-trump-pam-bondi-*and-25k-was-it-pay-play*

13. *insider.foxnews.com/2017/12/15/**pam-bondi**-robert-**mueller**-russia...*

14. *https://www.yahoo.com/news/trump-charity-gave-100000-to-david-bossies-citizens-united-that-helped-fund-lawsuit-against-moguls-foe-151337835.html*

15. *https://**talkingpointsmemo.com**/dc/**trump**-bondi-contributions*

16. *https://**www.nbcnews.com**/politics/white-house/**trump-failing-track**...*

17. *http://www.arbiternews.com/2017/03/09/trump-said-hed-donate-hotel-profits-heres-list-similar-promises-trump-hasnt-kept/*

18. *https://**www.politico.com**/story/2016/03/**trump-university-profits**-220595*

Chapter 6 Racism

1. https://**www.nytimes.com**/.../us/politics/donald-**trump-housing**-race.html

2. https://**www.huffingtonpost.com**/entry/donald-**trump**-racist-examples.

3. https://**www.nbcnews.com**/politics/2016-election/donald-**trump**-says...

4. *https://www.huffingtonpost.com/entry/donald-trump-racist-examples_us_56d47177e4b03260bf777e83*

5. *Ibid.*

6. *Ibid.*

7. *https://www.nytimes.com/politics/first-draft/2016/02/28/donald...*

8. *https://thinkprogress.org/trump-wants-less-scrutiny-on-violent-white-supremacists-685c3b0025ef/*

Chapter 7 Promises promises

1   Ryan Koronowski Twitter Apr 29, 2017, 1:37 pm

2   *https://www.washingtonpost.com/news/post-politics/wp/2016/01/22...*

3   ***www.politifact.com**/.../trumpometer/promise/1351/elimnate-common-core*

4   *https://www.washingtonpost.com/news/post-politics/wp/2016/01/22...*

5   *Ibid.*

6   www.lifenews.com/*2016/02/18/donald*-trump-promises-*as-president-i...*

7   *https://www.reddit.com/r/trumptracker/comments/5d7sn3/trump_never...*

8   *https://trumptracker.github.io/cut-the-budget-by-20-percent-by...*

9   https://www.washingtonpost.com/news/post-politics/wp/2016/01/22...

10 https://www.projectrepublictoday.com/2017/04/29 /president-trumps

11 reverbpress.com/finance/trump-outsourcing-jobs-report

12 www.politifact.com/.../promise/1412/declare-china-currency-manipulator

13 www.foxnews.com/politics/2017/04/12/trump-says-wont-label-china...

14 https://www.cnbc.com/2016/12/29/what-it-means-if-trump-names-china...

15. www.breakingchristiannews.com/articles/display_art.html?ID=21224

16 https://thinkprogress.org/donald-trumps-100-days-of-broken-promises...

17 Ibid

18 www.newsmax.com Politics/**Trump**-regret-remarks/

19 www.politifact.com/.../trumpometer/promise/1410 /renegotiatenafta

20 www.politifact.com/.../trumpometer/promise/1343/enact-term-limits

21 https://trumptracker.github.io/strengthen-the-military-so-that-its..

22 https://www.sbs.com.au/news/here-are-76-of-donald-trump-s-many...

23 www.cnn.com/2015/12/02/politics/donald-trump...

24 www.dailymail.co.uk/...fire-Internet-shutdown-calls-disrupt-ISIS.html

25 abcnews.go.com/Politics/donald-trump-bring-back-waterboarding/story?id=35354443

26 https://www.newsmax.com/Headline/Trump-University-Lawsuit-Settle/...

27 *https://*www.usatoday.com/*story/news/2016/11/18/
reports*-trump-*nears*...

Chapter 8 Hillary

1. *https://***www.washingtonpost.com**/*news/post-
politics/wp/2016/10/09/*...

2. **thehill.com**/*.../307210*-**trump**-*i*-**dont**-**want**-*to*-**hurt**-*the*-
clintons...*email*

3. **www.foxnews.com**/*politics/2017/11/03/***trump-slams-
sessions-doj-for**...

Chapter 9 Taxes

1. https://www.forbes.com/sites/janetnovack/2016/10/02/trump-
reported-916-million-tax-loss-in-1995-suggests-he-paid-no-
income-tax-for-years/#aea4852741b5

2. Ryan Koronowski Twitter Apr 29, 2017, 1:37 pm

3. **thehill.com**/homenews/administration/85237-**cbo**-estimates-
huge...

Chapter 10 Immigration

1. *https://***www.washingtonpost.com**/*news/the-
fix/wp/2018/01/09/we-got-a*...

2. https://**www.reuters.com**/article/us-usa-trump-immigration-
norway/

3. https://**trumptracker**.github.io/**deport-the-almost-11-
million**...

4. https://www.cnn.com/2015/08/19/politics/donald-**trump-
birthright**...

5. *https://***www.washingtonpost.com**/*politics/***trump**s-anti-
muslim...

6. *Ibid.*

7. **journalstar.com**/refugees/*article_8e026ad6-5ee0-5a9f-
90ab-55ffa0734*...

8. **www.politifact.com**/*truth-o-meter/article/2015/nov/24/donald-***trumps**...

9. **www.chicagotribune.com**/*news/nationworld/politics/ct-donald-***trump**...

10. www.politifact.com/*.../trumpometer/promise/1440/*triple-ice-enforcement

11. *https://***www.washingtonpost.com**/*news/post-politics/wp/2016/01/22*...

Chapter 12 The Wall

1   *http://www.cnn.com/2017/08/03/politics/trump-pena-nieto-call-transcript/index.html*

2   https://www.nytimes.com/2017/01/06/us/politics **/trump-wall-mexico**.*html*

3   *https://***www.cnn.com**/*2017/01/25/politics/***mexico**-*president-donald*...

4   *https://***www.washingtonpost.com**/*world/national-security/***you-cannot**...

5   *https://***twitter.com**/*realdonald***trump**/*status/ 953948941674078208*

Chapter 13 Obama Care

1. *https://***www.adn.com**/*politics/article/here-are-76-donald-***trump**s

*https://***www.washingtonpost.com**/*news/the-fix/wp/2018/01/17/sen*...

Chapter 14 Drain the Swamp

1. **www.city-data.com**/*forum/politics-other-controversies/2876550-what*...

2. **www.businessinsider.com/jared-kushner**-*ties*-**george-soros**-*goldman*...

3. **www.breitbart.com**/*big-government/2017/05/02/report*

4. **www.newsweek.com/jared-kushner**-*disclosure-form-west-bank...*

5. *https://***www.americanbanker.com**/*news/leaked-memo-alleges-widespread*

6. **www.latimes.com**/*politics/la-na-pol-trump-***mnuchin**-*price-20170926*

7. *https://***www.nytimes.com**/*2017/10/05/us/politics/***mnuchin** -*military*

8. **www.latimes.com**/*politics/la-na-pol-trump-***mnuchin**-*price-20170926*

9. *Ibid.*

10. **www.bbc.com**/*news/world-us-canada-38654226*

11. *www.washingtonexaminer.com/***trump-budget-director-nominee-failed-to...**

12. *www.allthatsfab.com/articles/news/***trump**-*closes-out-***his-first-year...**

13. *https://***www.nytimes.com**/*2017/01/18/us/politics/***confirma tion...**

14. *https://***www.huffingtonpost.com**/*entry/***scott-pruitt-**poultry...

15. *Scott Pruitt***www.latimes.com**/*politics/la-na-pol-trump-***mnuchin**-*price-*

16. *20170926indabusiness.com/news/view/9759/***carl-icahn-trump-adviser**-*red-flags...*

17. *https://***www.cbsnews.com**/*news/***rex-tillerson**-*is-no-fan-of-russia...*

18. *https://theintercept.com/2017/01/17/homeland-security-pick-gen...*

19. **www.latimes.com**/*local/lanow/la-me-***bernhardt**-*vote-20170724-story.html*

20. *https://theresponsibleconsumer.wordpress.com/national-campaigns/...*

21. **www.businessinsider.com/michael-flynn**-*charged-with-lying-to-fbi...*

Chapter 15 Little lies

1. http://www.pensitoreview.com/2017/06/25/trumps-100-lies-january-21-to-june-21-2017/

2. *Ibid.*

3. *https://***www.washingtonpost.com***/news/fact-checker/wp/***2017***/01/30/...*

4. *Ibid.*

5. *https://www.washingtonexaminer.com/trump-lays-out-case-for-extreme-vetting-for-middle-eastern-immigration/article/2613122*

6. *https://qz.com/555535/heres-how-refugees-are-selected-vetted-and-settled-in-the-united-states/*

7. *https://www.washingtonpost.com/?utm_term=.a982f3ca60a1* ***(cost cutting F-35 program)***

8. *https://www.nytimes.com/interactive/2017/06/23/opinion/trumps-lies.html*

9. *http://www.miamiherald.com/news/nation-world/world/americas/cuba/article165450707.html*

10. *https://***www.politico.com***/story/2017/01/***trump***-calls-the-***new-york***...*

11. **www.politifact.com**/*truth-o-meter/statements/***2017***/***feb***/06/donald...*

12. *https://***www.huffingtonpost.com***/entry/donald-***trump***-administration...*

13. **www.politifact.com**/*.../donald-trump-wrong-***murder-rate-highest-47-years***

14. https://www.washingtonpost.com/?utm_term=.a982f3ca60a1 **(F-35)**

15. *https://***thinkprogress.org/trump***-briefed-***flynn***-not-briefed-***flynn***...*

16. *http://fortune.com/2017/03/29/president-trump-job-claims-fact-check/*

17. *https://qz.com/555535/heres-how-refugees-are-selected-vetted-and-settled-in-the-united-states/*

18. *https://***www.politico.com***/story/***2017/02/***trump***-twitter-attacks...**(obamacare coverage)**

19. ***https://www.nytimes.com/interactive/2017/06/23/opinion/trumps-lies.html***

20. **Ibid.**

21. ***Ibid.***

22. *https://www.washingtonpost.com/?utm_term=.a982f3ca60a1* **(F-35)**

23. *https://***www.politico.com***/story/***2017/02/***trump***-twitter-attacks...**(obamacare coverage)**

24. https://www.washingtonpost.com/?utm_term= .a982f3ca60a1 **(F-35)**

25. ***https://www.nytimes.com/interactive/2017/06/23/opinion/trumps-lies.html***

26. https://www.washingtonpost.com/?utm_term= .a982f3ca60a1 **(F-35)**

27. *Ibid.*

28. ***https://www.nytimes.com/interactive/2017/06/23/opinion/trumps-lies.html***

29. ***Ibid.***

30. *Ibid.*

31. *Ibid.*

32. *Ibid.*

33. https://www.washingtonpost.com/?utm_term=
    .a982f3ca60a1 *(F-35)*

34. *https://www.nytimes.com/interactive/2017/06/23/opin
    ion/trumps-lies.html*

35. *Ibid.*

36. *Ibid.*

37. *Ibid.*

38. *Ibid.*

39. *https://www.washingtonpost.com/?utm_term=.a982f3ca60a1
    (F-35)*

40. *https://www.nytimes.com/interactive/2017/06/23/opin
    ion/trumps-lies.html*

41. *Ibid.*

42. *https://www.washingtonpost.com/?utm_term=.a982f3ca60a1
    (F-35)*

43. *https://www.nytimes.com/interactive/2017/06/23/opin
    ion/trumps-lies.html*

44. *https://www.washingtonpost.com/?utm_term=.a982f3ca60a1
    (F-35)*

45. *https://www.nytimes.com/interactive/2017/06/23/opin
    ion/trumps-lies.html*

46. *Ibid.*

47. *https://www.washingtonpost.com/?utm_term=.a982f3ca60a1
    (F-35)*

48. *Ibid.*

49. *https://www.nytimes.com/interactive/2017/06/23/opin
    ion/trumps-lies.html*

50. *Ibid.*

51. *Ibid.*

52. *Ibid.*

53. *https://www.washingtonpost.com/?utm_term=.a982f3ca60a1* **(F-35)**

Chapter 17 Russia Collusion

1. *https://**www.washingtonpost.com**/news/politics/wp/2018/0 1/11/trump...*

2. Specifically, as early as March 2016, Vladimir Putin had ordered an influence campaign against Hillary Clinton and in favor of Donald Trump in the run for President. [2]
    2*https://**www.nytimes.com**/2017/01/06/us/politics/russia-hack-report.html*

3. *https://**www.salon.com**/2017/05/28/**a-timeline-russia-and-president**...*

4. *https://**www.cnn.com**/2017/01/16/politics/donald-**trump**-times-bild*

Chapter 18 Self-funding his campaigning

1. *https://**www.usatoday.com**/story/news/politics/onpolitics/20 16/06/23/...*

2. https://www.huffingtonpost.com/entry/donald-trump-self-fund_us_57fd4556e4b00c1fb2b023e0

3. Ibid.

4. https://www.huffingtonpost.com/paul-heroux/is-tr ump-really-self-fina_b_9378228.html

5. https://www.huffingtonpost.com/paul-heroux/is-trump-really-self-fina_b_9378228.html

6. https://www.nytimes.com/2016/06/22/us/politics/donald-trump-self-funding-payments.html

7. http://fortune.com/2000/04/03/what-does-donald-trump-really-want/

Chapter 21 *1984*

1. https://www.politico.com/magazine/story/2016/05/donald-trump-2016-contradictions-213869#superComments

2. *Ibid.*

3. *Ibid.*

4. *Ibid.*

5. *https://**www.cnn.com**/2018/01/06/politics/trump-**genius**-tweet...*

6. *6https://boldanddetermined.com/donald-trump*

7. https://www.politico.com/magazine/story/2016/05/donald-trump-2016-contradictions-213869#superComments

8. *Ibid.*

9. *Ibid.*

10. *Ibid.*

11. *Miami Herald May 2, 201711https://www.spectator.co.uk/2016/07/donald-**trump**-is-making-america...*

12. **www.miamiherald.com**/*news/politics-government/election/donald-**trump**/...*

13. ***www.sun-sentinel.com**/local/palm-beach/fl-**two-trumps**-emerge...*

14. **thehill.com**/.../272666-**trump-there-are-two-donald-trumps**

15. *https://**www.washingtonpost.com**/blogs/right-turn/wp/2016/04/27/i-am...*

16. *https://**www.youtube.com**/watch?v=tggTv_TLoeY*

17. *https://**www.politico.com**/magazine/story/2016/05/donald-**trump**-2016...*

18. **time.com**/*4140698/donald-**trump**-interview*

19. https://**www.newyorker.com**/.../*25/donald*-**trumps-ghostwriter-tells-all**

20. *https://**www.politico.com**/magazine/story/2016/05/donald-**trump**-2016...*

21. *https://**www.politico.com**/magazine/story/2016/05/donald-**trump**-2016...*

22. -25.*Ibid.*

26. *https://**www.newsmax.com**/Newsfront/Donald-**Trump**-Ronald-Kessler/**2012**/...*

27. *https://**www.cnn.com/2015/07/24/politics/**
trump-illegal-immigration...*

28. **www.chicagotribune.com**/*news/nationworld/politics/ct-donald-trump*...

29. *https://**www.washingtonpost.com**/news/the-fix/wp/2017/08/28/timeline...*

30. *https://**finance.yahoo.com**/news/trumps-1990-playboy-interview...*

31. **www.politifact.com**/.../*2016/*...*down-what-donald-**trump**-thinks-about-abo*

32. *https://**www.factcheck.org**/2016/05/**whats-trumps-position-on-nato***

33. *https://**www.buzzfeed.com/andrewkaczynski/in-2002-**donald-**trump-said**...*

34. **thehill.com/blogs/ballot-box/presidential-races**
/270083-trump-day...

35. **www.politifact.com**/.../*trump-repeats-wrong-claim-he-opposed*-iraq-war

36. *https://**www.cbsnews.com/news/face-the-nation-transcripts-june-5***...*

37. *https://www.nbcnews.com/.../what-donald*-trump-s-position-libya-*n586141*

38. https://www.nbcnews.com/meet-the-press/video/ trump-*in-1999-i*-am...

39. *https://www.washingtonpost.com/news/the-fix/wp/...*

40. *https://www.politico.com/magazine/story/2016/05/do nald-trump-2016...*

41. https://*www.politico.com/magazine/story/2016/05/donald-trump-2016-contradictions-213869#superComments*

42. – 204. *Ibid.*

Acknowledgements

Thanks to Susan Wright of *Resurgent* and formerly of *Red State* for her insightful summation of my book in her foreword. Thanks again to my cousin, Donald Dorfman, Attorney in Sacramento for his encouragement after reading several chapters. Thanks also to Sharon Corbett Marsch, a Bosse High School classmate for her read and suggestions; to Renee Haag for her editing of some early chapters, to Lori Goshert for her read and comments on two chapters and to Brian Prince for some internet research on Trump. Thanks to Chris Watkins CPA for her review and suggestions for my chapter on taxes, and to David Cholesterol for the chapter on fake news. Also, thanks to all who submitted ideas for the Trump-speak glossary. There were so many that I couldn't use them all; but these are the people who made the grade: Scott Stavrou, for kleptocracy and nepotism; Leo James, for xenophobia; Janet Wright, for quack and universe; Beth Carroll Armstrong, for journalists; Sharon McGiness, for justice; and Christiana Doucette, for useless.